# The
# Great Dan Patch
## and the
# Remarkable
# Mr. Savage

# The Great Dan Patch

### and the

# Remarkable
# Mr. Savage

# Tim Brady

NODIN PRESS

Acknowledgements: Many thanks to Publisher Norton Stillman and Editor John Toren. Also thanks to Chuck Erickson, Jens Bohn, Janet and Will Williams, the Dan Patch Society of Savage, George Augustinack, Tausha Chamberland, the Savage Public Library, the Minnesota Historical Society Library, Beth Dale, Gregory Lind, Mary Phyllis Colwell, Dylan Savage, Dean Hoffman, and *Hoofbeats* Magazine.

Special thanks to Paul Bergly:
Almost one hundred years ago, M. W. Savage had the foresight to film Dan Patch in action, and thus preserve moving images of the great horse for all time. In the accompanying DVD, Paul Bergly has taken this rare and historic footage, combined it with period music written in honor of Dan, and created a delightful look at the horse, the International Stock Food Farm, and M. W. Savage.

ISBN 13: 978-1-932472-40-0
ISBN 10: 1-932472-40-1

Cover and layout: John Toren

Nodin Press is a division of Micawbers, Inc.
530 North Third Street
Suite 120
Minneapolis, MN 55401

A portion of the proceeds will go to the Dan Patch Historical Society, an organization which has championed the memory of both Dan Patch and M. W. Savage.

*To Susan, Sam, and Hannah*

# Table of Contents

# Foreword

On a sunny afternoon in the summer of 1906, ninety-three thousand people walked, rode, drove, or took a train to see Dan Patch put on an exhibition at the Minnesota State Fairgrounds. Even today such a hoard would be considered remarkable. No stadium in Minnesota can hold that many people. But Dan Patch was no ordinary horse. He was the greatest pacer of his time. In fact, some enthusiasts consider Dan Patch to be the greatest horse of ALL time. Dan Patch did not set any records that day in 1906, but he returned to the track the following Saturday and set a pacing record that stood unchallenged for more than three decades, and was not significantly lowered for half a century.

The story of Dan Patch's career is interwoven with that of his owner, M. W. Savage. Savage bought the horse in 1902 for the then remarkable sum of $60,000, but he knew what he was doing. Savage used Dan to promote a line of animal feeds, tools, and domestic items that ran to thousands of items. His International Stock Food Company employed hundreds of people and distributed products world-wide. Dan Patch was known to farmers and city-folk throughout the United States, many of whom had never been outside their home county. He was America's first sports superstar.

Savage used his famous horse as an advertising tool, and also built an impressive stock farm on the banks of the Minnesota River south of Minneapolis, based largely on Dan Patch's reputation on the race track. But by all accounts the bond between owner and horse went much deeper than a description of such merely commercial relations can suggest. The same can be said of the love felt by the many racing fans who crowded the grandstands at tracks from Toronto to Phoenix to see the horse perform. Dan was a sweetheart of a horse, and everyone knew it. He had won America's heart, and on the day he died the nation mourned.

Though harness-racing continues to draw a crowd in many parts of the country, other sports have encroached a good deal on its popularity. And though a town on the Minnesota River still bears the name Savage, nothing remains of the lavish stock farm that was once its pride and joy. Yet a phenomena of such staggering impact is unlikely to be entirely forgotten, and the legacy of Dan Patch has been preserved by racing enthusiasts in Minnesota, in Oxford, Indiana (where Dan was born and where he first raced) and in locales throughout the country where collectors avidly buy and sell the watch fobs, straight razors, tobacco tins, and wheel barrows that bear the Dan Patch name. The towns of Savage and Oxford have both long since revived the spirit of their most famous "citizen" by means of a yearly Dan Patch festival. And in 1991 the fans of Dan Patch in Savage brought their collective expertise together to form the Dan Patch Historical Society, which is dedicated to preserving the heritage of the horse and his owner, and also to expanding our appreciation of those larger-than-life events and times.

We were very pleased, therefore, to learn that seasoned author Tim Brady would be turning his attention to this fascinating chapter in America's history, and we lent both our personal insights and our extensive archives to the project. The story of America's first sports superstar, and of the never-say-die entrepreneur who brought his image into the barnyards and onto the dinner tables of families from California to Connecticut, deserves to be retold, and Tim Brady has told it well.

– Jens Bohn, President

The Dan Patch Historical Society

Hennepin Avenue looking north, ca 1903

# Prologue:

## *The Spirit of the Times*

It was the first Monday of the New Year, 1903, and the city of Minneapolis was primed for the new day and a new era. A symbol of that fresh start was scheduled to arrive at the Union Depot that morning—a newcomer who would bring to Minneapolis and the whole state of Minnesota a type of fame and prestige neither had known

before. Groups of well-wishers thronged down Nicollet and Hennepin
Avenues toward the station on the Mississippi River, hoping to catch a
glimpse of the pilgrim as he stepped off the train from Kansas City. The
Minneapolis Journal's "Newsboy Band" was also on hand to escort the
dignitary to his new upscale digs on Portland Avenue, along with the
swells from the Minneapolis Riding and Driving Club, who'd arrived at
the depot in stylish rigs pulled by what had been, up until that historic
morning, the cream of Minnesota's harness racing horses. Eventually,
more than three thousand sports fans and horse-lovers gathered around
the train station where the celebrity was about to disembark.[1]

Minneapolis was a bustling town with or without this anticipated
arrival. The city had grown at a remarkable rate in the preceding two
decades, from 40,000 to more than 200,000. Newcomers, primarily
from Germany and the Scandinavian countries, joined the Yankee
entrepreneurs who had founded the city, and its economy boomed.
Flour mills sprung up on both sides of Saint Anthony Falls, the only
cataract on the entire length of the Mississippi River. The harvested
grains of western Minnesota and Dakota farms poured into the city
to be ground into a silky flour and bagged under labels that quickly
become household names, like Pillsbury Gold Medal. The wheat was
shipped to eastern markets in such quantities that Minneapolis had long
since earned the nickname The Mill City and was acknowledged as the
flour capital of the nation.

The power supplied to the mills by the falls also fuelled a thriving
lumber industry. In fact, sawmills clung to the banks of the river like
barnacles, creating such a porridge of sawdust and timber scraps below
the falls that navigation on the river was hazardous. Aside from being
the nation's number one flour miller, in 1903 Minneapolis was also its
greatest producer of lumber.

The Great Northern Railroad, which snaked into Minneapolis
from its home base in Saint Paul on the beautifully curved Stone Arch
Bridge, represented the final essential element in the area's economy.
The chief carrier of passengers and freight from the Upper Mississippi
to the Pacific Northwest, it was owned and operated by the state's most

renowned figure, James J. Hill, and played a central roll in the region's development as a transportation hub.

The Stone Arch Bridge

Yet for all its burgeoning industry, growing population, and civic and cultural improvements, Minneapolis remained something of a frontier city. Though it was striving to escape its provincial image, Minneapolis was "Western" in the late nineteenth century sense of the word, meaning not only that it was that part of the United States that didn't include the East Coast and the states of the Confederacy, but that it was rawboned and rough around the edges. Many of its citizens took pride in the fact that they—or more often their parents, the first generation of Euro-American Minnesotans—had forsaken the comforts of the East for a more vigorous life on the prairie. All the same, it was difficult to escape the uncomfortable feeling of being on the very fringes of the world that mattered. Those who reflected on Minneapolis's place in the nation were all too aware that the centers of the financial, political, and social universe were east of the Mississippi—and they weren't thinking of their twin city rival, Saint Paul, in this regard.

The sons of the elite went to New England for their higher education and toured Europe to soak up the culture. Aside from James J. Hill, a St. Paulite, there simply weren't many figures of national renown in the area. The region had already gained a reputation as the country's icebox and seemed an appropriate new home for the Scandinavian refugees who'd been streaming into the state from Europe's own frozen climes in recent decades.

To add to the sense of provincial discomfort, Minneapolis had recently become notorious throughout the nation as a result of a scandal involving its mayor, Dr. Albert Ames. In the late spring of 1902 a grand jury had met to consider charges against the amiable but corrupt city leader, and before long Lincoln Steffens, the famed muckraking journalist, had arrived in Minneapolis to cast his critical eye on the situation. In just a few months time, the disgraced and indicted mayor would be on the lam from the law, traveling incognito as tales of his misdeeds became known to the public, and Steffens' article detailing the corruption, "The Shame of Minneapolis," would appear in *McClure's*, one of the most widely circulated magazines of the day.[2]

Ames was the son of one of the pioneer physicians of Minneapolis and had first been elected to his office in 1880, when the city was clustered on either side of the river at St. Anthony Falls. By the time Ames had been elected for a fourth time in 1900 (they were non-consecutive terms), Minneapolis had grown into a thriving urban center with all the problems that come with rapid growth, a transient population and a small constabulary. Vice flourished, and Dr. Albert Ames was not the man to rein it in.

According to one historian, "Ames was a tall, handsome, kindly man, but [he] had his weaknesses. He drank too much and was easy to wheedle. Doing a favor to a friend meant more to him than being honest." These character flaws became more and more evident as the man's tenure in office increased, and by the time the century turned, "the better angels" of Ames' nature were fully submissive to the weaker. He decided that "the public attention and prestige that the mayor's office had previously brought him" was no longer a good enough reason to helm the city. As his fourth term began, "he wanted money, too."

In order to collect this graft in relative freedom, Ames proceeded to fire half the city's police department and appoint his brother, Fred Ames, as Chief of Police. Fred had just returned from less than distinguished service with the army in the Philippines, where he had been accused of cowardice and had nearly been court-martialed. Nonetheless, Fred was now the chief law enforcer in Minneapolis, and assigned to assist him as captain of the police force and chief detective, respectively, were the owner of a notorious coffee-house named "Coffee John" Fitchette and a former gambler named Norman King. A medical student named Irwin Gardner also came on board to oversee one of the administration's most lucrative vice divisions: the cities "disorderly houses."

Minneapolis, like most cities in the era, had official proscriptions against establishments of ill repute, even as they allowed them to exist in certain areas of the city. In Minneapolis, the "patrol lines"—the boundaries between the "good" side of the city and the "bad"—ran along the riverfront. Within them were the opium joints, unlicensed saloons (called "Blind Pigs"), and houses of prostitution frequented by the denizens of the underworld. Across town, Minneapolis proper went about its business with a quick stride and a blind eye toward the illicit trade.

Among the innovative schemes of the Ames' crew was to force prostitutes to buy illustrated biographies of city officials. To help conceal the true nature of their houses, it was suggested to several ladies that they open street level candy stores, from which they "sold sweets to children and tobacco to the 'lumber Jacks' . . . while a nefarious traffic was carried on in the rear." Owners of the "Blind Pigs" were forced to buy tickets to the games of the police baseball team.

Peddlers and pawnbrokers who had previously been licensed by the city now got their papers directly from the mayor's office, and Ames and company pocketed the fees. Slot machines were made legal and 200 were set up in locations across the city. Ames split the take with machine owners and garnered $15,000 in the bargain. Thieves and confidence men streamed into the city, according to Steffens, operating freely, with a wink and a nod from the city's police, who took a cut of the take.

These and a long list of other transgressions came out during the course of the Grand Jury proceedings throughout the summer of 1902.

By the time the jury handed down its indictments, Irwin Gardner and Fred Ames were under lock and key, and Albert Ames had skipped town to avoid the same. To the credit of Minneapolis, all of this had been exposed by the end of the year, and a new administration was now being sworn in at City Hall with promises to reform the politics of the city. Unfortunately for area boosters, the January issue of *McClure's* hit the newsstands at the same time, and people all over the country were relishing the details of Lincoln Steffens' expose with its provocative title "The Shame of Minneapolis."

## The Depot

Yet down at the Union Depot that January morning, all that the gathered well-wishers knew or cared to know was that a genuine celebrity was coming to town by way of the Omaha Road. A champion was moving in to make a permanent home in the tundra, riding in the comfort of his own special car, decked out courtesy of the American Express Company. Here was a nationally recognized sports star, whose shine was about to help illuminate the whole region.

Never mind that he was a horse. Never mind that Dan Patch had yet to race his most brilliant miles. Never mind that he had been competing on The Grand Circuit of harness racing, the sport's premier venues, for just two years, and that none of those tracks were in Minnesota. Never mind that he had never set foot in the state and that only a handful of those who had come to see him at the depot had ever seen him race. Horse racing fans everywhere knew about Dan Patch. They knew that he was not only the best pacer in the nation, but that he was so good, he couldn't find any horses to race with him. In fifty-six starts, he'd only lost twice, and those were heats; and in one, it was said that his driver had let up so that the competition wouldn't be too intimidated by the sheer speed of him.

In a land crazy for sports, the arrival of Dan Patch was news, not just in Minneapolis, but in sports pages across the country—comparable to the day, some seventeen years later, when Babe Ruth was sold by the Boston Red Sox to the New York Yankees. But this four-legged celebrity wasn't headed toward any metropolis—he was headed for the hinterlands.

Dan Patch had been the talk of the harness racing world for much of the past year. He'd had a spectacular season on the circuit, which was quickly followed by rumors of his impending sale. Then, on December 8, 1902, it was announced that Marion Willis Savage, owner of the International Stock Food Company of Minneapolis, Minnesota had plunked down $60,000 to a New York horseman named M.E. Sturgis for the rights to Dan Patch. Negotiations had been in the works for weeks but weren't capped until Myron McHenry, Dan's trainer and driver, came north from Kansas City for a face to face talk with Savage.

"I have purchased Dan Patch largely to use for exhibition purposes," Sav-

**M. W. Savage**

age announced to the papers the day after their meeting. "Mr. McHenry is under contract to drive him two years more, and will therefore continue in charge of the horse.

"Dan Patch has made a mile in 1:59 ¼ but the record has been disputed, and he is generally given but 1:59 ½ , which is fairly good, I guess," Savage said, with studied understatement. "Since there is no horse left for him to go against, Dan Patch will be tried out on various tracks, and Mr. McHenry believes that under favorable conditions he can reduce his record to 1:57 flat."[3]

No one had ever paid $60,000 for a pacer. And the fact that McHenry was coming with Dan made it all the more special to Minnesotans. To many, McHenry was as classy as the horse, and it was a favorite subject of dispute in the world of harness racing, whether it was Dan Patch himself or Dan Patch with Myron McHenry at the reins who were invincible.

To racing fans, the times that Savage referred to so dryly also meant a great deal. It might be a horse-and-buggy world, but that didn't mean people didn't crave fast horses and fast buggies. Beneath the masthead of the oldest sports journal in the country, the banner read, "The spirit of the times is speed," and there would have been few on Nicollet Avenue that January morning who disagreed. Ever since a harness horse named Yankee had broken a three-minute mile in a race in Harlem, New York, way back in 1806, time had been an obsession of harness racers. Horses were not simply designated by their names; attached to the moniker was the fastest time they'd ever run in the mile. Dan Patch was not just Dan Patch. He was Dan Patch 1:59 ¼.

And the fact that it was the dawn of a New Age in Transportation— a time when backyard inventors across the country were tinkering with automobiles that they hoped would carry them from point A to point B in a blink of an eye, the same year that the Wright Brothers would be the first to succeed at powered flight, a year in which there were already three hundred automobile owners in Minneapolis—only whetted appetites for horse speed. It might have been the dawn of a new era but the streets of a typical American city were still jammed from morning until nighttime with a cavalcade of horse-drawn vehicles, everything from beer wagons to rag carts to fancy phaetons and carriages. Traffic was a disaster, the pace of business glacial. Vehicles moved in fits and starts, and it was no simple matter for a team of horses to negotiate the streets of urban America. A fully-loaded dray needed two minutes or more to cover one city block, and when it backed into the curb to unload its merchandise, all traffic in the street, horse drawn and foot, would come to a halt for minutes at a time as the team slowly shifted into reverse.

Dan Patch could haul a driver a full mile in less time than it took for that dray to slowpoke its way down a single city block. To the crowd down at the depot, that was a solid feat, and they could easily dream of speeding down Nicollet, leaving the slow motion world of the nineteenth century behind, as they were pulled in a flying sulky by the likes of Dan Patch.

Down at the station, the fans waiting for the horse to arrive in his private car from Kansas City were hanging from the bridge above the rail yard and standing in the snow near the tracks down below. Up on Nicollet they waited, too, until finally, from the south, they heard the whistle of the train. There is no record of the gossip that was exchanged when the car finally appeared in the distance or as the horse's car was slowly unhitched and switched into the depot. But when the brakes had hissed for a final time, when the car came to a last halt, and the handlers slid the car door open, "The crowd surged up into the door of the car in such numbers, that several minutes were required to clear the way sufficiently to bring out the horse."[4]

## Hello, Dan Patch

If Dan Patch's head was turned by all this attention, it was hard to judge by the look of him. In fact, he was bundled so tight against the Minnesota cold that few were able to get a peek at his features at all as he clip-clopped down the ramp set against the rail car. They could see he was a mahogany-colored stallion, and many knew his height and weight—sixteen hands and just under twelve hundred pounds— from the ubiquitous stories written about him in the newspapers. They also knew that he was six years old, soon to be seven; but all attempts to get a good long look at him were futile, and to ascertain his state of mind was speculation. Not that that stopped people from guessing.

Using a trope that would become familiar in the life of Dan Patch, the next day the *Minneapolis Journal* published a mock interview with the just de-trained horse: "'I should have preferred to enter the city quietly, without any of this brass band racket,' said Patch. 'This public reception business always bores me and in fact I dislike all newspaper notoriety . . .'"

The *St. Paul Pioneer Press* was a little more traditional in ascribing Dan's mood: "Dan Patch evidently felt very fine after his long journey, a fact probably accounted for by the assiduous care with which his attendants watch every move he makes. No young dandy of the Cashbags aristocracy ever had more attentive body servants than Dan has, while his nonchalant acceptance of every attention indicates that he has been well brought up—with proper comprehension of the divine rights of kings."

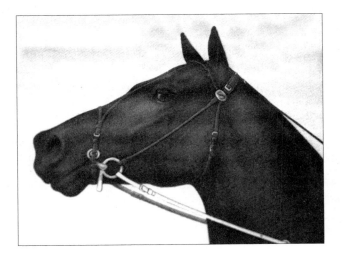

All eyes were riveted on Dan as he marched down the plank and onto the station platform. Members of the Minneapolis Riding and Driving Club were gathered together, with their horses well-groomed and shiny, like a latter-day contingent of NASCAR buffs in their gleaming hot rods. As noted by a writer from the *Minneapolis Tribune*: "When the handsome brown horse made his appearance there was a chorus of whoops from the assembled spectators, while the rank and file of the equine racing contingent braced up to look pretty as the champion went past."

Meanwhile, Savage was giving his own statement to the press, describing what the upcoming weeks and months would hold for his new purchase. After wintering in Savage's stables in town, the horse would be taken to green pastures on the Minnesota River, where Savage and his International Stock Food Company had established a stock farm unlike anything that had been built before in the country. In addition to a mile-long track constructed by the best harness-course designer in the country, the farm had great rows of stables radiating from a central pavilion, which was topped by a domed turret. The eastern flavor of the structure had already earned it the nickname The Taj among locals, who'd been viewing its construction throughout the fall and winter.

"My great desire is to show the horse world that we can breed harness racers in Minnesota," Savage said. "Many men expressed the opinion that it was suicidal to bring Dan Patch to this state, but I see no reason why we should not breed just as good light harness horses as any other state, and in two or three years I believe my theory will be proven. Millions of dollars are poured into the state of Iowa every year as a result of the development of breeding in that state, and surely the climate there is not materially different from ours. It will take time to demonstrate our theory, but when we prove it, it will mean a great deal for the state."

## Man of Mystery

Without a doubt, M. W. Savage was the most excited person to see Dan Patch that morning. In fact, it was the first time he and his $60,000 purchase had ever laid eyes on one another.[5]

Later accounts, more fanciful but less accurate, had Savage lurking about the stables and tracks of the Grand Circuit through much of the autumn of 1902, "a man of mystery" silently appraising Dan Patch until he finally decided to reveal himself and make his $60,000 bid to M. E. Sturgis. An *Esquire* magazine article, written long after the events, describes Savage as "a quiet, soft-spoken man in frock coat and derby" who trailed Dan Patch around the circuit, "holding a stop watch" to time Dan in his paces. According to this legend, Savage, at the track, was "deaf to gambler's tips. He neither smoked nor drank, and he never visited the track on Sunday. The stable boys took to calling him The Parson."

In truth, Savage had no need to personally inspect the horse. Not only was Dan Patch's reputation and record impeccable, but Savage had good horsemen in his employ to check the pacer out. These included the trainer Harry Hersey, who ran Savage's stables in Minneapolis, and Robert Fremont "Fish" Jones, the secretary of the Minneapolis Riding and Driving Club. Jones was probably the premier authority on harness-racing in Minnesota. He had been the one to assume the responsibility of organizing the parade to honor the arrival of Dan Patch.

In fact, by the time the Man of Mystery purchased Dan Patch, he wasn't much of a mystery to the world of harness racing. With Hersey's help, M. W. Savage had made three high-profile purchases of championship harness racers in 1901 and 1902, all with the well-publicized intention of establishing a world-class stable in Minnesota. Nor was Savage "parson" material. While it was true that he was a devout Methodist and a man who neither drank nor smoked, Savage had a certain flair suggesting that whatever piety was contained within him was matched by an equal dose of capitalist fervor and plain showmanship. John Hervey, the greatest harness racing writer of the day, had a vivid recollection of meeting Savage for the first time, months before the Dan Patch purchase. "His personality at once arrested me," Hervey wrote. "He was a slightly built man of medium height, stylishly but not flashily dressed, unusually good-looking and of very pleasant address, though with the air of a self-made man who was sure of himself ... I saw at once that he was no ordinary individual through a stroke of luck pushed into the limelight, but a truly unusual man."[6]

Savage had been in contact with Sturgis since early in 1902 about Dan Patch. At that time, the horse had been just one year on the Grand Circuit, but already the talk in horse circles suggested he was something special. "Rumors that Dan Patch was the coming champion pacing stallion were heard on every hand," Savage later recalled. "His wonderful speed was the talk among horsemen and I commenced to study over the problem of securing him for my International Stock Food Farm. In the spring of 1902,

I telegraphed Mr. Sturgis that if he decided to sell Dan I would be pleased to have the first chance and his reply gave me some encouragement."

All of this was the culmination of a long-held dream for Savage. The son of a country doctor and patent medicine man from Iowa, he was forty-four years old when he landed Dan Patch for his new farm. Savage had arrived in Minneapolis from Dubuque about fifteen years earlier, with little more than his own ambition and a few chemical recipes culled from his father's trade. But while Dr. E. W. Savage had devised medicinal prescriptions for human consumption, his son, "Will" Savage, made similar concoctions for livestock and grew remarkably successful in the process.

It wasn't so much the recipes that brought him success, however, as his ability to sell them. Savage turned out to be a brilliant marketer, a man of the future in regards to his salesmanship, and Dan Patch was about to become his most spectacular selling tool.

In years to come, the name and shape of this horse would be familiar to every fan and farm family member in the nation. Millions would glance at his image daily on the bucket of feed they lugged around the barn or on the wall by the kitchen table as they sat down to supper beneath the homely Dan Patch portrait supplied by Mr. M. W. Savage and the International Stock Food Company. They would do their laundry in Dan Patch washers, stick plugs of Dan Patch chewing tobacco between their cheek and gum, and glance at Dan Patch pocket watches as they rode Dan Patch wagons home from the feed mill, loaded with Dan Patch International Stock Food supplements, hoping to get home in time for supper, which would be served on Dan Patch dinner plates.

For all the fame that the pacer brought with him to Minneapolis that morning, it was nothing like that which was about to rain down. Dan Patch had started a journey down a path that no athlete in

American history had ever traveled before, from renown to super stardom, and Will Savage was holding the reins.

The bonus for Savage was that he was a man who truly loved horses and had done so all his life. "Many people have thought the purchase of Dan Patch was a sudden rash impulse that came over me when I was in an 'advertising' frame of mind," he would write later. "How far this is from the truth, the following statement will show: I was born with a great desire to raise high-class harness horses."

## Down Nicollet

With a crew of mounted police up ahead to keep the streets clear and The Newsboy Band playing, the procession headed from the depot toward downtown Minneapolis with "Fish" Jones in the lead, followed by Dan Patch "so covered with blankets that only a very vague idea could be secured of his points." In the district just off the river called "Bridge Square," the parade veered to the left and headed down Nicollet Avenue rather than Hennepin, which held the city's trolley cars and was considered less conducive to parades.

Jones presumably took the lead because he'd organized the parade and was the sort of man who loved to lead them. He was a well-known character in town: a race promoter and editor and publisher of a magazine devoted to horses, the *Northwestern Horseman and Stockman*. Jones had arrived in Minneapolis in 1876 from New York and had soon established a thriving fish market on Hennepin Avenue, thus earning his nickname, which he loathed. Among a number of eccentricities, including a penchant for always wearing a silk top hat because of his height (or lack of it), Jones kept a variety of exotic fish and aquatic life, first at his business and then at his home, also on Hennepin Avenue (on the present site of Minneapolis's Basilica of St. Mary). In time, his interest in sea life expanded into earthbound critters and his menagerie became the basis for the first zoo in Minneapolis's history.[7]

Following Jones, the band, and the horse down Nicollet Avenue was the proud owner, M. W. Savage, and Harry Hersey, who would be put in charge of caring for the animal—and whose story would soon be as tightly linked to Dan Patch as anyone's. The horses and drivers from the Minneapolis Riding and Driving Club brought up the rear.

Paved and lit by gas streetlights, Nicollet was the city's premier retail thoroughfare. Here were the city's finest department stores—Powers, Goodfellows (soon be known as Dayton's), and Donaldson's, a five-story structure made almost entirely of glass and iron, with fourteen separate departments. In the 500 block of Nicollet, the parade passed the one retailer in the city selling ready-to-wear women's clothing: Young Quinlan's, a store founded by Elizabeth Quinlan, a former star saleswoman at Goodfellows.

An impressive mix of well-heeled gentlemen in fur-collared coats and ladies in big hats were on hand to watch the great stallion pass. No doubt there were a few rougher customers, too, perhaps some denizens of the Blind Pigs and "candy stores" down by the river. But despite the exuberance of the crowd and the boisterous sound of the band, the parade marched at the pace of a heavily blanketed horse who had just completed an exhausting train ride from Kansas City. Puffs of frozen air drifted up from Dan Patch's nostrils. Mittened hands applauded as he walked down the street. There were shouts of "Go get 'em, Dan."

Eventually the party veered off Nicollet toward Portland and continued south toward Marion Willis Savage's impressive home on Portland Avenue, a Queen Anne period mansion, only five years old. Two turrets covered towers on opposite ends of the house, and a pair of porticos received guests from both Portland and Twenty-sixth Street.

No one knows just how much of the crowd accompanied the horse all the way to his new home, though it's likely that Jones and the Driving Club stayed with the procession, as well as the most deeply devoted harness racing fans among the pedestrians. Perhaps a pack of street urchins raced ahead of the procession to get a front-on view of Dan Patch loping toward them, then raced ahead again as he passed.

This would not be the last time that Dan Patch made this parade from a custom-made railroad car down Nicollet Avenue to his city home. Year after year he would make the same pilgrimage, following another season on the harness racing tracks of America. Parades would soon become old hat to the horse and his handlers, an event lived many times over, in towns all over the country. Dan Patch would pull into the local station, be met by admiring fans, and paraded to the nearest fairgrounds or racetrack or the best stable in town. And everywhere the expectation was the same: that at the end of the day, this tired horse, just off the train, would go faster than any harness horse they'd ever seen. Rarely did Dan Patch disappoint.

Toward the end of his career, however, the more prescient in the crowd may well have recognized that a changing of the guard was near. Even as they walked this horse to his next race, they would have understood that the culture of horse travel itself was near an end, that the automobile had changed everything, and that Dan Patch would soon be history. But even the most foresighted of this bunch would have been shocked at how quickly the revolution would come.

Ten years after his death, the life of Dan Patch would seem irrelevant to all but devoted harness racing fans. Thirty years after his death, he would be a symbol of harmless nostalgia resurrected by Hollywood as an emblem of a simpler time, the details of his life lost in a happy image of a rural America powered by horses clip-clopping down country lanes at a howdy-neighbor pace. A century down the line, he would be remembered primarily as a collectible, a faded image of nostalgia plastered on odds-and-ends found on eBay and in antique stores.

But in his day, Dan Patch was a symbol of vitality and glamour. He was about big parades and racetracks set right next door to the barkers at the midway on the state fairgrounds. He was about the value of horse-flesh in a culture still very much driven by those animals. He was about the promise of fast times in hick towns, salesmanship, and the mix of urban and rural worlds in the changing American landscape.

More than anything else, Dan Patch was all about the tick of the clock—all about the speed.

Dan Patch's first stable in Oxford, Indiana

# 1

# Dan's Debut

Dan Patch was foaled in 1896 in Oxford, Indiana, a town located in the west-central part of the state, about halfway between Indianapolis and the Illinois state line. Dan's owner, Daniel Messner, was the proprietor of a local dry goods store and a novice at raising horses. In fact, he bought Dan's mother Zelica only because his doctor recommended that he get out of the store more often and get some fresh air on a Sunday drive or two. At the time of the purchase Messner didn't even have a stable in which to board his new acquisition.

According to later accounts, Dan Patch's hind legs were so crooked at birth that he couldn't stand on his own to be nursed by his mother, and neighbors talked disparagingly about the mahogany-colored colt. But from the beginning, Dan showed the pleasant disposition that would become a trademark throughout his racing career.

Dan Patch's pedigree, though not remarkably different from that of other obscure harness horses of the time, did contain many links to Messenger, the grand patriarch of American harness racing horses. In fact, through Zelica, his mother, Dan Patch was linked to Messenger through twenty-one different lines of relatives going back nine generations. Through his sire, Joe Patchen, an additional twenty-two links could be identified, giving Dan a family tree with forty-three branches going back to Messenger in one way or another.[1]

The issue of bloodlines had not been a matter of much concern during the early days of American harness racing, but as the sport developed enthusiasts began to notice that an unusual number of championship horses could claim ancestry with Messenger. The *American Stud Book* would eventually confirm that every distinguished trotting horse that had raced in the region of New York, New Jersey, and Philadelphia in the first half of the nineteenth century was descended from Messenger, who had arrived in Philadelphia back in the days when the United States Constitution was being debated in that city.

Messenger had had a brief and successful racing career in England, but he had fallen into obscurity by the time he disembarked in the City of Brotherly Love in 1788. He lived on into the nineteenth century, however, standing for stud service in Pennsylvania, Long Island, upstate New York, and New Jersey. He was already well-known for producing quality "gaiters" long before he died, and it was a matter of widespread amazement that such a horse—a non-trotter—could transmit a perfect trotting gait to so many of his offspring. The word standardbred (as opposed to thoroughbred) was eventually coined to describe Messenger's many eminent descendants, and this appellation for harness horses continues to be used today.

Despite her links to Messenger, Zelica's ancestry was far from spectacular. She had been sired by a horse named Wilkesbury, who was thought to have potential as a racer but never got a chance to prove it. He was drowned in a swollen creek when the carriage he was tied to overturned in the rushing water. Zelica herself was injured early in her life and wound up going in just one race. She lost that start.[2]

On the other hand, Dan Patch's sire, Joe Patchen, not only had links to the great Messenger, but was a fine pacer in his own right. When Zelica was brought to him, he had just finished an outstanding season as a six-year old on the Grand Circuit, dropping his best time from 2:19 ¼ to 2:04. By the turn of the century Joe Patchen would be considered one of the great stars of the circuit, reaching a best time of 2:00 ¾, which placed him among a handful of the fastest harness horses of his day. He was also, according to many accounts, a horse with a temper—a quality which he probably picked up from his own sire, another fine horse named Patchen Wilkes.

A friend of Messner's, a horseman named John Wattles (who was still training horses at the age of seventy), had suggested that Zelica be taken to Patchen, who was stabled across the state line in Chabenese, Illinois. The $150 fee seemed steep to Messner, but he eventually agreed, and away went his mare with Wattles to the stud. A few months later, on April 29, 1896, Dan Patch was born.

Dan's early experience on the track was typical of standardbred horses everywhere at that time. Before being introduced to the trotting and pacing gaits, he was first broken to saddle and then jogged over the dirt roads around Oxford, where he quickly displayed an instinct for pacing. Dan's racing days still lay far ahead of him, however. Unlike thoroughbreds, standardbreds in those days were rarely raced until they were three or four years old. Hiram Woodruff, the premier driver and trainer of the era, had observed in his 1870 guide to harness racing that in days gone by, trotters were not even taught the gait until they were five years old, but in his more modern era, it was perfectly acceptable to begin training at two.

Dan was given over to Wattles for training in his third spring. Oxford legend had it that a local blacksmith fashioned an extra-wide sulky to accommodate the wayward kick of Dan's curved legs. Wattles took the horse to a half-mile track two miles east of Oxford and worked with him through the spring and summer. Horsemen in the region must have seen some measure of speed in the colt early on: though he'd yet to race in competition, Messner turned down offers of $1,000 in both 1898 and 1899 for the young pacer.

Years later, Oxford natives would relate their distinct memories of watching Dan train and would describe details of his cooling-down walks after his exercise. All recollections suggest that Dan had an amiable disposition from his earliest days—as did Mr. Messner—and neither was averse to letting the boys of Oxford hitch a ride on the back of Messner's sleigh during the Indiana winters.

The particulars of Wattles' training methods for Dan Patch are lost, but in his influential book Hiram Woodruff encouraged the gradual training of a horse, insisting that a gaited horse not be rushed toward speed in his workouts. "He must be carefully watched to ascertain whether he improves or not. If not, he is to be let up a bit; for his improvement at this age [three] ought to go on all the time, and will if he is all right."

Messner used Dan as his "driving horse" as soon as the colt was old enough to assume that chore. The owner liked to smoke a cigar on these trips and would occasionally let Dan participate in brushes on the country lanes around Oxford.

## Dan's Debut

In August of 1900 Messner and Wattles finally decided it was time to unveil Dan Patch to a racing audience. They chose the Benton County Fair for Dan's debut, in the county seat of Boswell, near Oxford, and the setting couldn't have been more appropriate for a horse like Dan. Though the sport had first blossomed on the well-traveled highways of the East Coast and in particular in New York City; it was in midwestern towns like Boswell, and at county fairs like this one, that it continued to flourish in the last quarter of the nineteenth century. Its origins as a sport "of the people" made it a natural for these venues. Nearly everyone in an Indiana county came to visit the fair, and according to accounts in the Oxford paper, all stores in town closed for the event except for the post office.

A dollar fifty got an entire family into the Boswell fair for the full five days of agricultural displays, homemaking exhibits, midway

Daniel Messner (left)
and John Wattles

amusements, and harness racing. Visitors were advised to come early
to avoid the midday dust and grime that was inevitably kicked up by
all the traffic. The grandstands filled early, too, and a choice seat cost
extra.

Thursday, August 30, was Dan's debut at the fair and rumors about
his speed were already widespread. Those who had seen him training
over the past year thought they were witnessing something special, and
one observer had timed him at a local track doing a mile in 2:14, which
was a Grand Circuit-level performance.

Boswell had a half-mile track, and Dan was entered in the
2:35 class. The best three out of five heats took home the prize. The
seventy-year-old Wattles was chosen to drive Dan Patch, which seemed
appropriate. Here was a living link to the sport's past, driving the horse
that would define its future in the new century. According to eye-witness
accounts, Wattles wore a blue silk cap and a jacket trimmed with gold.
But the outstanding aspect of his appearance was his long white beard,
which was parted down the middle and flowed behind him as he and
Dan Patch sped around the track. In fact, one spectator, pressed many
years later to recall the historic moment—the first race of the great Dan
Patch—could only picture that beard.

And so, looking like some Old Testament prophet riding a chariot to battle, Johnny Wattles drove Dan Patch around the half-mile circuit at Boswell. They took the first heat in 2:24 ½. They took the second heat in 2:22 ¼. They took the third heat again in 2:24 ½, and the word from Wattles was that he could go much faster than that.

In an era when hundreds of thousands of people prided themselves on knowing what a good horse was, thousands of Indianans felt they knew a little better than most. Almost all of them who were gathered at Boswell that day felt the same thing: they'd just seen a very special horse.

## Moving On Up

As a result of his performance, the buzz about Dan Patch's prowess quickly grew louder and more fervent. Crowds poured into the Lafayette, Indiana, track the very next week for Dan's second go, and even after he lost his first heat (one of just two such defeats in his entire career), enthusiasm for the horse wasn't dampened a bit. He had started in a second-tier position and was "pocketed" behind a horse named Milo S. Dan Patch was only able to show his true speed down the stretch, when he got clear of the rail and started to cruise past all his competition. Unfortunately, he lacked sufficient time to catch the leader. That was the consensus of observers, anyway, and to prove them right, Dan quickly swept through the next three heats with a 2:16 best time.

In two more starts that September—one in Crawfordsville and one in Brazil—no horse seriously challenged Dan Patch, and it was apparent to his fans that he was far better than the competition at the fairs and local races of west central Indiana. When the season was over Messner pondered what his next step ought to be, and quickly decided that Dan was ready to perform in the Grand Circuit, the major league of the harness racing world. But to do so he would need more professional training and driving.

Enter Myron McHenry.

In 1900 Myron McHenry was considered by many to be the best reinsman in the country, and he was in peak form. His nickname on the racing circuit, "The Man From Freeport," was something of a misnomer since he was actually from a northern Illinois town named Geneseo (he'd recently purchased a farm near Freeport). A Methodist like Will Savage, but with far fewer pieties, McHenry and his father, a local church leader,

McHenry driving Dan Patch, ca 1901

had an early falling out over the son's interests in horse racing. McHenry debuted as a driver in 1880, but his father made no effort to see him at the reins until thirteen years later at the 1893 Chicago World's Fair.

By that time, McHenry was recognized as one of the best drivers on the Grand Circuit. He had trained and driven Mable A, Phoebe Wilkes, and the great John R. Gentry 2:00 ½ (a rival of Joe Patchen). He also became the only man in history to breed, train and drive a Kentucky Futurity winner, Rose Croix.[3]

No one knows why this Grand Circuit giant agreed to train and drive Dan Patch for the 1901 season. There is no evidence suggesting that McHenry had actually seen Dan Patch race at that time. Evidently Messner simply wrote to McHenry and asked him. One observer of events adds, "Mr. McHenry thought little of the Oxford postmark and remarked that every horse owner in the 'sticks' thought he had a winner if his horse showed the least amount of speed."

Perhaps the fact that Messner had both the money and willingness to pay McHenry sealed the deal; yet it seems unlikely that McHenry would agree to the job without seeing Dan Patch's quality or having assurances of it from some racing expert whom he trusted. In any event, in March 1901 Messner announced to his neighbors in Oxford that the great Myron McHenry would be driving Dan Patch in the Grand Circuit the following year.

Dan would be scheduled to appear in Detroit; Cleveland and Columbus, Ohio; Buffalo, Glen Falls, and Syracuse, New York; Readville, Massachusetts; Providence, Rhode Island; Hartford, Connecticut; Terre Haute, Indiana; Lexington, Kentucky; and Nashville, Tennessee. The local horse was about to hit the big time.

# 2

# Harness Racing: A Backward Glance

arness racing had arisen from informal beginnings on the highways of colonial America. It was given a boost when a number of legislatures in the northern states of the new nation, dismayed by the environment of crime and gambling that almost invariably grew up around thoroughbred racing, passed laws closing area race tracks.

Harness racing was not generally viewed in quite such a dismal light. After all, thoroughbreds were galloping horses, and galloping horses were, by definition, horses bred for speed. The horses used in harness racing assumed a more genteel gait that was less threatening to those who opposed tracks and gambling. A trotter moved at a measured speed in a particular style designed for smooth transportation, with diagonally opposed legs moving together at the same time, right front with left rear and then left front with right rear. "The theory was if a horse was trotting," wrote harness racing historian Philip Pines, "he obviously was not going as fast as he could if he were running."[1]

Trotting horses were usually carriage horses with a different work ethic, body style and bloodline than thoroughbreds. Their legs were shorter and their bodies were longer. They weren't as sleek and pretty as thoroughbreds; and they served other purposes in life than to simply go fast.

Despite this common sensibility about trotters, their owners were not immune to the racing impulse. During the early decades of the nineteenth century, trotters began to meet one another on the highways of the northeastern states with increasing frequency for impromptu "brushes." When no competition was available, horses were simply timed to see how fast they could go. The expanding network of roads connecting the growing cities of the region, especially those between Boston, New York, and Philadelphia, not only made for good carriage travel, it also gave trotters and their drivers new opportunities to test their speed. After all, it would be difficult for legislators, however straight-laced, to close a track that was also a public thoroughfare. And in fact no authority was overly concerned to put its foot down on the seemingly harmless past time.

The informality of these early harness races stood in stark contrast to the stylish veneer of thoroughbred racing, with its emphasis on blood lines, hired riders, and sport-of-kings traditions. The first open-road trotter drivers were the James Deans of their day, meeting on the highways north of New York City for a go down the straight stretch above Harlem Village.

Such brushes could range anywhere from one to five miles in length, and they usually took place on roads where taverns were located at convenient intervals. The driver was carried behind his horse in a two-wheeled carriage that had room for only a solitary rider, on which account it was called a sulky. The drivers almost invariably owned the horses they raced, and the animals themselves were typically not pampered thoroughbreds but functional steeds, who would be called upon to drive their bosses home after being raced all afternoon.

The popularity of these informal competitions soon led to efforts to organize them, and the movement to turn harness racing into an orthodox sport was given a boost when several states began to liberalize their anti-racing legislation. In 1823 the state of New York allowed a harness race to be held on Long Island before a public audience. About two years later, the New York Trotting Club (NYTC) became the first official harness racing club organized in the United States and was soon followed by an association in Philadelphia.[2]

The loosening of anti-racing legislation eventually allowed thoroughbred racing to return to northern states, but its popularity was dampened by a downturn in the nation's economy. In any case, during the period when race tracks had been outlawed in the north, racing enthusiasts had been reminded that harness horses were less expensive to keep than thoroughbreds and served more purposes for their middle-class owners. They were also more durable than thoroughbreds, could race a longer season, and remained competitive for many more years than their pampered cousins. And because they were both more durable and less glamorous than thoroughbreds, race promoters found that they were obliged to pay less in prize money to harness racers, which also helped the sport to survive and even prosper during hard times.[3]

Trotters were also far more numerous than thoroughbreds. Any local farmer with a good, fast driving horse could head for the track or the straightaway and test his mettle against the nearby competition. In this way, good trotters could and did emerge from humble beginnings. Perhaps the most famous harness horse of the antebellum era, Lady Suffolk, was four years old and pulling a butcher's cart when she was discovered by a horseman named David Bryan. Bryan bought the horse and proceeded to race her more than 160 times, right up until her death in 1851 at the age of 19.

Though it became more organized with the passing decades, trotting remained a sport conducted by men with few airs. Its traditions were flexible and accommodating to spectators, and its races were conducted in a wide variety of styles and distances. At the same time, as the popularity of the sport increased, harness racing enthusiasts began to take a greater interest in aspects of the business that had hitherto been the exclusive domain of thoroughbred racers. The sport was becoming organized.

## The Growth of Harness Racing

Harness racing boomed in the years just prior to the Civil War, spreading across the Midwest into the small towns of Ohio, Indiana, Michigan, Illinois, Iowa, and Wisconsin along with the advancing tide of settlers. Press coverage of the trotting game increased, too, and more money began to flow into the sport. Big buck horsemen like Robert Bonner, owner of the *New York Ledger*, and famed capitalist Cornelius "Commodore" Vanderbilt made owning trotters a respectable past time for the elite of New York society.

Bonner was a strait-laced Scotsman, and like Dan Messner, he had first taken an interest in horses in response to his doctor's recommendation that he get more fresh air and exercise. He spent large sums of money on a stable that included some of the premier horses of the day, including Maud S. and Pocahontas, for which he paid $40,000 apiece.

Bonner shared the views of an earlier generation that race tracks were cauldrons of sin, but he loved to race his fine trotters on the highways of New York, most especially up Harlem Lane. It was here, in the 1860s, that he and Vanderbilt initiated a legendary series of races that would pit their best trotters against one another for years.

General Ulysses S. Grant, one of the most passionate horsemen of the day, was also seriously attracted to trotting. In November 1865, on a visit to New York just months after accepting Robert E. Lee's surrender at Appomattox Courthouse, Grant drove the famed horse Flora Temple (the inspiration for the "bob-tailed nag" in the song "Camptown Races") against Vanderbilt and Bonner. He lost, but his love for the trotters remained strong. In subsequent years Grant was often seen with a cigar in his mouth, jogging Bonner's horses on the streets of New York City.

With its increasing popularity and an infusion of money from owners like Bonner and Vanderbilt, harness racing began to take on the veneer of a modern sporting enterprise. In the 1860s the National Trotting Association (NTA) was formed to create a governing body for the sport. Representatives from forty-six tracks in fifteen states met in New York to discuss such matters as a unified handicapping system, which would ultimately determine a horse's quality by its best time in the mile.

Prior to the formation of the NTA, complaints of cheating and fraud were widespread, and bribes and fixed races were common occurrences. One commentator labeled the cheaters Sharps and their victims Flats and suggested that the greatest benefit of organizing the sport would be to break the control of the drivers over turf affairs and place it in the hands of judges. The sport's origins on empty stretches of highway had given it the anarchic spirit of a playground basketball game, where the players call their own fouls and referees were nowhere to be had, but those quaint days were largely over. In any case, the NTA was needed to bring some authority and fairness to the higher levels of competition.

## Trotters and Pacers

The Grand Circuit, the tour upon which Dan Patch would soon be performing, was established in 1871 as another link in the chain of the sport's modernization. It was formed when track owners from Buffalo, Springfield, Massachusetts, and Cleveland gathered in Ohio to discuss the feasibility of organizing an association. It took a couple of years and the addition of a few more tracks to get the organization up and running, but when it was, the Grand Circuit helped to standardize racing formats and coordinate competitive scheduling at quality tracks.

During its early years the Circuit did not consider pacing a harness racing sport worth promoting. In fact, for most of the nineteenth century pacers were not in vogue, though the roots of this prejudice had become obscure by the time Dan Patch raced. Robert Bonner was quoted as saying, "No gentleman drives a pacer," but just why that should be so he did not elaborate.

Pacers were otherwise known as amblers, sidewheelers, wigglers, sandsifters, double-shufflers, kangaroos, or "the poor man's trotter," nicknames deriving from the peculiar way a pacing horse moves. A pacer moves both legs on a given side in tandem, left front and left rear, followed by right front and right rear, shifting its body back and forth with each step in a lateral motion. Trotters, on the other hand, move like most babies crawl: right front and left rear legs move forward together; then left front and right rear.

The nature of the sport required that in competition a horse must assume the particular type of gait appropriate to the race. Break the gait, and a horse must fall back until he or she regains the appropriate trotting or pacing motion. In the nineteenth century, trotting aficionados tended to view pacers as "quitters." A trotter who broke his or her gait in a race was quick to change back again and continue with the race. Pacers, on the other hand, were thought to break more often and had more difficulties resuming the pace.

Pacers, though they were often looked down upon, had speed equivalent to, if not better than, trotters, and in the Midwest, they were always popular starters in county fair races. Individual pacers like Oneida Chief, Hero, Pocahontas, James K. Polk, Tecumseh, and Longfellow had done well racing against trotters, but few of the most serious horseman in the mid-nineteenth century were interested in training or breeding pacers.

It was the popularity of pacers in the small towns of Ohio, Michigan, and Indiana which finally convinced the Grand Circuit to open its doors to pacers on a major scale. In 1878, Cleveland track owner Colonel William Edwards staged what was called "a free-for-all" race at his Grand Circuit track, and four horses, Sleepy George, Bay Sallie, Sweetser, and Lucy, emerged as stars from this event. Over the next few seasons, other pacers joined these horses as stars on the circuit, and a memorable series of races, featuring a new Big Four—Lucy, Mattie Hunter, Rowdy Boy and Sleepy Tom—drew large crowds on the circuit, and the races were made all the more compelling by the fact that Sleepy Tom was completely blind.

Tom, a grandson of the great Pocahontas, had been owned and trained by a driver named Stephen Phillips. Phillips sold him, and Sleepy Tom drifted from one abusive owner to another, losing his eyesight at some point in this miserable journey. At the age of twelve, he was rediscovered and re-purchased by Phillips, who decided to re-train him for the harness circuit in the state of Ohio despite the horse's handicap. In just a year's time, the horse was back to championship caliber, and in 1879, at the age of thirteen, he was pushed by Mattie Hunter to a world's record in the mile—2:12 ¼—exceeding the mark set by the trotter Rarus by a full second.

A blind horse breaking a world's record was good stuff, and the racing public lapped it up. Pacing had finally come of age as a legitimate part of the harness racing scene. In 1878 only one horse in thirty on the harness racing circuit was a pacer; seven years later the ratio had dropped to one in nine; and in 1892 it was one in five. Though prize money for pacers continued to lag the trotting fields and pacing remained more popular in the Midwest than the East, there was no denying the quality of the horses and the competition.

Other pacing stars emerged in the 1880s, like Johnston, a gelding with an untraced pedigree bred by a German farmer in Wisconsin. In a career that anticipated Dan Patch's in many aspects, Johnson broke the world's pacing record in 1883, outraced all his competition, and wound up being sold to a Minneapolis man named Commodore Kittson, who raced him in exhibitions for the remainder of the decade.

The 1890s brought new stars to the pacing circuit with the brilliant careers of Hal Pointer and Direct. Direct was a California horse from the stable of a legendary trainer named Monroe Salisbury. He was born from a line of trotting horses but was trained as a pacer. Five years old when he started his first race, he'd come east in 1891 to challenge the best on the Grand Circuit, and halfway through the season, he'd toppled Johnston's mile record by a quarter second, setting a new standard at 2:06.

Hal Pointer was from Tennessee and lacked the sleek lines of the California horse but was a favorite of his home state crowd. Pointer had beaten all rivals for three straight seasons on the Circuit, including Johnston, who had returned from retirement expressly to challenge him.

The stage was set for a memorable race between Direct and Hal Pointer, and the pair raced against one another in Terre Haute, Indiana, in 1891, with the Tennessee horse winning in a thrilling series of heats. Just a few weeks later, however, Direct came back to whip the native son in three straight tries at Memphis, and he confirmed his superiority later that month at races in Columbia, Tennessee. Again, the focus of the harness racing world was drawn to the pacing class, further enhancing its growing popularity.

The fear that a pacer would break his or her gait and come to a halt during a race remained ever-present, but in the mid-1890s a device called a "hopple" became available that helped to minimize this problem. A hopple was a leg harness that forced pacers into their proper gait. The harness had been used to train pacers for many years, but its appearance on the racetracks further signaled the growing acceptance of pacers as legitimate competition to trotting horses. In fact, Star Pointer, the first horse to break the two-minute mile in 1897, and arguably the most famous harness horse in the country at the time, was a pacer.

By the time Dan Patch made his debut on the Grand Circuit in 1901, pacers were viewed by many fans as every bit as worthy of attention as trotters. And Dan's career would leave no one in doubt about the matter.

Cresceus 2:02 ¼

# 3

# The Grand Circuit

Dan Patch began his 1901 season with a warm-up race at Windsor, Ontario. It was July 10, and one turf writer, getting his first look at the five-year-old, described him as "a rugged looking stallion with the best of feet and legs ... He has a bold way of going, very much like his sire, although not gaited like him behind. His manners are simply perfect."[1]

Dan faced his first real competition that day in Windsor—a quality pacer from the Rocky Mountain region named Winfield Stratton. If Dan Patch felt any nervousness about beginning a career in the big time of harness racing, he didn't show it. Dan swept the three heats of his first truly competitive race with an impressive 2:07 best.

The following week in Detroit, for his inaugural go in a Grand Circuit race, Dan was made a 5-to-1 favorite on the strength of his showing in Windsor. He easily took his three heats in a contest with so little challenge that it was labeled "featureless" in his biography. A week later, with the same odds and similar competition, his race was called "no more than a stiff jog." And in Columbus, Ohio, at the end of July, "Dan went a nice work-out race" and swept again with a 2:10 ¼ best.

At that time Dan Patch's press coverage was just a fraction of what it would later become, making detailed descriptions of his early races hard to come by. But it's evident that he was turning heads on the Grand Circuit, just as he'd turned heads in Indiana. In fact, John Hervey asserted that in just three weeks on the Circuit Dan had become the most-talked-of young pacer in America, and already he was the prohibitive favorite in every race in which he appeared. [2]

In Buffalo, New York, on August 8, McHenry and Messner felt the need to do something different to keep Dan's victories exciting for the crowd. McHenry held Dan back in each heat until the head of the stretch, and then sent him down the home stretch with an electric burst of speed. [3]

Messner was no doubt feeling a few rushes himself. Purses for the four races Dan Patch had already won that summer totaled $9,000. The previous year in Indiana he'd been earning a piddling few hundred dollars per race. Dan Patch's value was skyrocketing, and it was rumored back in Oxford less than halfway through his first year on the Circuit that the stallion would soon be on the market. Messner was quick to deny such talk, and the season continued as Dan took his first spin at Brighton Beach.

This was the horse's inaugural race in New York City, and here were gathered the elite of the harness world, both in terms of horseflesh and human refinement. Though Dan was not the principal attraction—that came in the form of a match race between the famed trotter Cresceus and his rival, The Abbot—Patch was noticed, talked about, and admired.

One track writer described Dan as "fresh from five consecutive victories ... in which he had played with his fields." But at these earlier races, Dan met horses in slower classes—2:14, 2:15, 2:16—and now he was up against rivals in the 2:08 class, and the competition would be that much stiffer. Though he was a heavy favorite, some track observers felt that he might be vulnerable.

The New York race crowd was as sophisticated as any in the country. It had seen championship horses ever since trotting was introduced on the Harlem Speedway. Even so, one writer remembered seeing in Dan Patch a horse whose brilliance was apparent from a first glance: "I had heard so much of him, without seeing him, that when the chance came, I was among the first who formed the ring soon packed about him as he was made ready for the opening heat. He stood ... with an expression of innate power ... I felt that this horse, merely in repose, surpassed all [my] expectations."

Dan Patch was obviously an impressive horse, but here at Brighton Beach, for the second time in his career, he was defeated in a heat. Once again the race looked to many like a fluke, and it was subsequently reported that Dan was interfered with or that McHenry "preferred to lay up for the heat" rather than push his stallion. [4]

Another report cast McHenry in a less friendly light. Dan Patch was purposefully held back by McHenry, as this story had it, simply because he wanted to see the speed of the other horses in the race. In this version, McHenry's actions enraged fans, and an irate few threatened to lynch McHenry until the police were brought in to calm things down. The track stewards offered McHenry a stern rebuke, reminding him that Grand Circuit rules "obligated each driver . . . to drive his horse to the best of its ability." Properly chastened, McHenry let Dan Patch do his thing, and the horse quickly asserted himself over the field, sweeping the remaining three races, while achieving a personal best time of 2:04 ½ in the process.

At Brighton the most talked about race was run by the famed trotter Cresceus, who beat The Abbot in an exciting match. A race between a pair of pacers, Anaconda and Prince Alert, had also caused a stir. But Dan Patch also generated a lot of buzz racing for the first time in New York. The writer who had been so impressed with Dan Patch "merely in repose" remained astounded by the newcomer's talents. "What shall I say then, of the impression [Dan] produced when, after laying him up in the first heat, in order to ascertain the speed and temper of the field, he was cut loose in the second? It was, in fact, indescribable. As I think of it I can only recall the description, in some old romance, of some knight of invincible prowess as he swept through the tournament, scattering all who dared oppose him as a whirlwind scatters chaff."[5]

Rhetoric aside, Dan was obviously a talented horse and such a prohibitive favorite in the 2:14 class in his next races, at Readville, Massachusetts, and Hartford, Connecticut, that betting windows were closed. He swept both races, as well as a race at Providence at the end of August. At Cincinnati, on September 21, it was said that in winning, "he simply jogged along, enjoying the scenery and was not made busy in any part of the race."

The Cincinnati race was the closest venue to Dan's home in Oxford, and a contingent of home-towners were eager to see their boy race. However, the Oxford gang couldn't get a group rate from any of the railroads, so they let the opportunity pass.

After the Cincinnati race, Messner brought his horse home for a brief rest before finishing the season in Kentucky and Tennessee. It was on this trip home, with his wallet full of Grand Circuit winnings, that Messner leased "the finest residence in Benton County," where it was said around town that "Dan Patch ... would be a privileged guest in the parlor."

In Lexington, a horse named Shadow Chimes made a creditable attempt against Dan but couldn't catch him. On October 22, on a brand new track at Memphis, Dan raced for the last time that season. Aligned against him were a number of horses that he'd seen already on the tour, including Mazette, Harold H, and Major Muscovite. They were no more able to catch Dan in Tennessee than elsewhere.

As the season ended, an article in the *New York Times* listed all the trotters and pacers who were newcomers to harness racing's Honor Roll—horses who'd achieved times of 2:10 or better on the 1901 circuit.

Dan Patch, with his 2:04 ½ at Brighton Beach, was at the top of the list for pacers.

To horsemen with a keen eye, there was no doubt that he was a coming marvel. "It was not so much the fact that whenever he started it was Dan Patch 1-1-1; it was his individuality and manner of 'doing it,' that proclaimed his greatness," wrote Hervey. "He was born a racehorse, perfect in every spot and place."

"He could turn on anywhere in the mile," Hervey continued, "responding to McHenry's touch on the reins as if he were moving a lever in a machine; after a fast heat he pulled up as if from a jog, not breathing enough to blow out a candle."[6]

## Homecoming

The town of Oxford pulled out all the stops in welcoming its native son home, and on November 14 it staged the first recorded Dan Patch Day. The Oxford band led a parade around the town square playing a song composed just that fall by the band director, James W. Steele, in honor of the local hero. Called "The Dan Patch Two Step," it would be the first of several songs dedicated to the stallion.

Following the band, probably pacing in time with the music, was Dan Patch himself, who was quickly gaining a reputation for being at home in a crowd. "He seemed to know his townspeople did something out of the ordinary in his behalf," wrote Mary Cross in *The Two Dans*, "and kept looking around at his admirers as if he appreciated all the attention."[7]

Dan was followed by his mother, Zelica, and his first daughter, Lady Patch. Then came two half-brothers, Messner and Respond, who were followed by the Messner family.

Horsemen from all over the west-central part of the state were in Oxford to pay homage to the pacer, and they stayed for a church supper following the parade, where pumpkin pie and other home-made old-fashioned delights were served. The townsfolk were thrilled to have the king of pacers in residence, and there was plenty of speculation about what new milestones the next racing season would bring.

But like so many rural boys of the day, Dan's future lay in the wider world. His owner, Dan Messner, must have known that—and known that he himself was not the man to take Dan Patch to the highest heights.

Soon after Dan arrived home, one of his stable-mates was found dead, and poisoning was suspected. Though no one was ever charged with the crime and there was nothing to indicate with certainty what had actually happened, Messner felt that the incident was prompted by jealousy of his and Dan's success, and he worried about the safety of his champion horse.

Messner eventually became convinced that Dan Patch's future was best placed in other hands, and on March 1, 1902, he sold Dan Patch to Manley E. Sturgis, a sportsman from Buffalo, New York, for $20,000. The citizens of Oxford were heartsick, though Messner offered a list of reasons for the sale, including the tale of the poisoned stablemate. He also observed that: "Being in the dry goods and lumber business, I do not have the time to develop so many horses ... Because I still own his mother ... I think I can raise several Dan Patches."

Though this would turn out to be wishful thinking, Dan Messner was more than happy that his $150 investment had returned $20,000, and he was content to see his horse moving to greener pastures.

More than anything, Messner recognized that the horse that he'd raised from a wobbly-kneed colt to a champion racer had long-since outpaced the country life.

# 4

# The Sporting World

The last quarter of the nineteenth century ushered in a new era in the world of sports, as individuals and families with more leisure time began to take a greater interest in playing them, watching them, and following them, both in the daily newspapers and in an ever-increasing number of sporting journals that were being published to satisfy that need.

At the same time, technological advances expanded the range of sports coverage and made possible the creation of a truly national sporting scene. Scores and details of contests and games could be sent anywhere in a matter of moments by means of the telegraph, making up-to-date sports pages a fixture in many daily newspapers throughout the country. Newly-developed techniques for reproducing photographs brought sports heroes to life on the printed page. An increasingly urban population lapped up details of sporting events as never before.

The railroad network, weaving its way across the land, made it possible for local athletes and teams to compete against far-flung opponents, creating a national network of sporting events to match the widespread interest in their outcome. Baseball was no longer just a homespun product played in town parks on lazy Sunday afternoons, but a national past-time with big leagues, all-stars, and a World Series. College football grew from a rough form of campus entertainment into a seasonal passion for hundreds of thousands of fans, and since 1898 the sport had an "All-American" team chosen (with some partiality, in the view of a few western fans) by the Yale football coach, Walter Camp.

A remarkable array of sporting activities were either born or enhanced in the last years of the nineteenth century. Technological advances in bicycling led to a period of immense popularity for that sport in the 1890s, and also aided the development of the sulky, which by 1893 had adopted the improved pneumatic biking tire for use on the track.

In Springfield, Massachusetts, Dr. James Naismith had famously tacked peach baskets to the walls of the local YMCA, thus devising the soon-to-be popular game of "basket ball" as a winter amusement for the town's young recreationists. Tennis was gaining a large following, and from Scotland and the British Isles, golf was taking hold. Courses were being plotted and constructed in cities all across the United States.

Women, too, began to assert their rights to compete in sporting events. Basketball, bicycling, tennis, and golf were all popular with women at the turn of the century, and one writer was so enthused by the prospects of participating in sport that she wrote, "With the single exception of the improvement of the legal status of women, their entrance into the realm of sport is the most cheering thing that has happened to them in the century just past."[1]

Ancient sports like track and field and boxing were revivified as well. The modern Olympics were reconstituted in 1896, and boxing, which had always had its aficionados, now had one in the White House. Theodore Roosevelt, the nation's chief amateur pugilist, was also a tennis nut, and the country's principle philosopher and proponent of the republican value of exercise and the sporting life.

The popularity of harness racing actually predated this boom, but the growing interest in sporting events of all kinds did nothing to undermine its continuing appeal. At the turn of the century, there were 860 active harness racing tracks stretching across the continent from California to Phoenix to Dallas and north to Montana. Tracks could be found all across the Upper Midwest and down through Iowa, Nebraska, and Kansas to Oklahoma City. There were tracks in Memphis, Lexington, and Macon, Georgia. They were scattered throughout the Northeast and into Canada at Toronto and Windsor, and also throughout Michigan, Indiana, Ohio, and Pennsylvania. [2]

Driving clubs like the one that greeted Dan Patch's arrival in Minneapolis sprang up around the country during the 1890s as a means for amateur harness drivers to get out and test themselves and their horses against local competition. The afternoon races were called "matinees" and were a direct descendant of the "brushes" from which the sport had sprung. The amateur clubs also revived the use of four-wheeled wagons in harness racing—a form of competition that had once been common but had virtually disappeared from the track with advances in sulky technology.[3]

As with other sports that rode the boom in printing, word of racing was spreading everywhere through national journals like the *Spirit of the Times, Horse Review, Wallace's Monthly*, the *Breeder and Horseman*, and the *Western Horseman*, all of which covered horses and the tracks. Smaller journals like "Fish" Jones's *Northwestern Horseman and Stockman* satisfied the need for local news about all things horses, from racing to breeding to trading. And daily papers covered events at the tracks along with all the other sports.

By the spring of 1902, when he began his second season on the Grand Circuit, the name of Dan Patch was familiar to sports enthusiasts throughout the country. In a little more than a year he'd risen from the status of an obscure Indiana pacer racing at county fairs to national renown. For the many horse racing fans who had yet to see him pace, he was still only a name in the paper, but that name was already evoking the prospect of an exciting day at the track, should Dan Patch ever come within a reasonable distance of their local ovals.

The world was getting smaller, and the number of sports heroes celebrated and idolized throughout the country, including Dan Patch, was getting larger.

## The Price of a Pacer

M. E. Sturgis, Dan Patch's new owner, was a popular fixture in the New York horse world. He was a bachelor who moved comfortably in high society, sometimes in the company of a spinster sister. He was described by John Hervey as "urbane, pleasant-spoken and agreeable" with the look "of a prosperous banker." Yet he was also a professional gambler. "One might have spent interminable time in his society and never for a moment suspected that he was of the profession to which he belonged."

The *New York Times* preferred to call Sturgis a sportsman and declared that he was better known in trotting than pacing circles. When he bought Dan Patch, he already had a stable of quality trotters that he kept in New York City. His name appears frequently in stories of local horse shows and sales (a staple of newspapers and stock journals everywhere), and it was said that he was also a "well-known Speedway driver." The Speedway races were amateur "matinees," staged by the New York Driving Club. They had remained a popular past-time since the earliest days of city racing, though by the 1890s they had been booted off Manhattan's streets and out into Fleetwood Park.[4]

Though driving was in his background, Sturgis was not interested in taking Dan Patch's reins. "The Man from Freeport," Myron McHenry, remained in that position and also continued to train Dan that spring at the Empire City track in New York.

The 1902 season began in familiar fashion for Dan Patch. Once again, the stallion opened his racing season at Windsor, where he met Harold H, whom he'd beaten twice in 1901. Harold H was a Canadian horse and a favorite of the crowd at Windsor. It was widely felt that here on his own turf, Harold H could give the hotshot American pacer all he could handle, but the pace turned out to be too lively for the Canadian horse, and Dan Patch won the match in a jog.[5]

Dan then headed over the border to Detroit to race as a newcomer to the 2:04 class, which, with a pair of notable exceptions, was the cream of the 1902 pacing crop. Searchlight, Connor, and Indiana were matched against Dan Patch, and in the first heat, Searchlight led at the quarter-mile and half. On the backstretch, however, Dan Patch closed the gap effortlessly and won by two lengths, slowing up at the end. The second race in a best two out of three was less competitive, and Dan took home a purse of $1,500.

Five days later Dan Patch was in Cleveland, matched against the same three horses, plus Riley B. Once again, he swept three of three heats without much competition and again pocketed $1,500 for his owner.

At the same time, two horses that might have challenged Dan Patch, Prince Direct and Anaconda, were engaged in a series of match races against one another, which they would continue to stage through the fall. Precisely why neither horse chose to race Dan, or vice versa, in 1902 remains obscure, though the question would return, at least in the case of Prince Direct and Dan Patch, in the 1903 season.

As it was, just three races into the 1902 circuit, it was obvious that Dan Patch had no other competition in the 2:04 class. Searchlight, Connor, Indiana, and Harold H were all quality horses, but they couldn't hold a candle to Dan Patch. Rather than continue to flog the competition, Sturgis and McHenry decided it was time to match Dan against another competitor: for the rest of the season, he would race against the clock.

## The Exhibitions

Timed exhibitions by champion horses were not unusual occurrences in those days. In fact, there was a tradition of racing horses against the clock that stretched back to the days when horseracing had been outlawed in the northern states. The bootleg races that were held in lieu of officially sanctioned events included timed exhibitions. As historian Dwight Akers points out, "Racing was illegal, but there was nothing in the laws that forbade the citizen … to see how fast his horse could go." In fact, a horse named Yankee, the first trotter to be recorded as traveling a mile in under three minutes in 1806, did so in a timed trial. During the 1880s Johnston outraced his competition and went on the exhibition tour. [6]

To add sport to the trials, the exhibition horse would race against a specific time, and tracks would offer a purse for a successful race. Bettors, of course, would also have a chance to lose their money by wagering on whether on not a horse could top the posted challenge. Dan Patch's career in timed trials began at Columbus, Ohio, on August 2. The standard chosen was 2:01 ¼—the best time of his sire, Joe Patchen.

Before what was described as an immense crowd, Dan set out after his father's record. There were no strict rules at the time on how a speed exhibition ought to be staged. The featured horse would typically use a "rabbit" to spur him on. Called "runners," these speed horses would race ahead of the champion at a gallop, and the exhibition horse would give chase. That's precisely what happened at Columbus, and Dan sailed home in the oedipal mile at 2:00 ¾, beating his father's best mark by a half second.

Two weeks later at Brighton Beach in Brooklyn, Dan set out to break Star Pointer's world pacing record of 1:59 ¼. A full day of racing at the track was scheduled, including a match race between Prince Alert and Anaconda, but according to the *New York Times*, it was Dan Patch "in a race against 'Father Time'" which drew the biggest audience. About six thousand watched him attempt to break Star Pointer's record with two runners going ahead. An offer of $5,000 from the New York

Trotting Association for a new record was not incentive enough for Dan. Once again, he raced to a 2:00 ¾ finish.

The record was obviously in jeopardy, but Dan milked the drama. In Massachusetts at the Readville track on August 23, he took another half-second off his best time before a large crowd on the same oval on which Star Pointer had set the record five years to a day earlier.

In Providence, a week later, he became only the second harness horse in history to break a two-minute mile. *The New York Times* said his 1:59 ½ was raced "in a blaze of glory," but the fact that it was a quarter of a second behind Star Pointer's record and that it came in the midst of a series of marvelous runs, tended to detract from its greatness.

In Philadelphia, in early September, he hovered around two minutes but didn't crack the barrier. Thirty thousand came to watch him race at the New York State Fair in Syracuse, hoping he'd crack the two-minute mile again, but after a :59 ¼ half, he hit a breeze on the home stretch and had to settle for a 2:00 ¼.

Back in New York in the middle of the month, this time at the Empire City Trotting Club in Yonkers, Dan Patch's go for the record was the talk of the race world. "Dan Patch, 1:59 ½, the pacing wonder ... is as sound as a dollar," gushed the *New York Times*, on Sunday, September 14. But even with that endorsement and a prize of $5,000, Dan didn't have the record in him, and paced the mile in 2:02.

The next week, back at Readville, Massachusetts, Dan Patch, in a truly magnificent performance, finally equaled Star Pointer's record. The weather was nearly perfect, and Dan did a warm-up mile in 2:13, before setting out a half-hour later to make a run at Star Pointer's record. A runner was sent out ahead of him, and as Dan approached the starting wire strung above the track, McHenry nodded at the timers, signaling his horse's readiness for the run. According to the *Times*, "A hundred watches caught the start" as the pacer quickly hit his stride. There was not a skip in his pace for the whole mile, the *Times* reported, "his legs moving in perfect regularity," and at three-quarters of a mile, the crowd knew the record was in trouble. On the backstretch, Dan passed the runner and flashed under the wire in a time of 1:59 ¼, tying the five-year-old world record of Star Pointer. The crowd went wild and so did the harness-racing world.

"The greatest of the year's performances in harness unquestionably was the record-equaling mile by the stout young pacer Dan Patch at Readville, Massachusetts on September 23," the *Times* reported a week later in a review of the season's harness racing. "After chipping fraction after fraction from his own record in many races against time and working to the point of triumph by quarter seconds, [Dan Patch] finally finished a mile in exactly the same time as the old world's record of 1:59 ¼ made Star Pointer on the same track five years before."

There would be more attempts to break Star Pointer's record that fall—in Terre Haute, Davenport, and Cincinnati; and finally on a year-ending southern tour to Memphis—but Dan Patch's best race of the season had been run. Despite the fact that he hadn't quite topped Star Pointer, few were disappointed.

"The majority of admirers of Dan Patch are content with the honors that the great horse has won so far," said the *Times*, "especially as they are more than confident that he has it in him to beat the old by a margin sufficient to leave no room for dispute."

The *Minneapolis Journal* was slightly more cautious. "Dan Patch may succeed in his task of beating Star Pointer's and his own mark next year ... He may show even better form next year than he has this summer." But for any horse to break a record, the paper said, "wind, weather and track would have to be perfect." The point was well-taken. Even for a great horse like Dan Patch, opportunities to break records would be relatively few.

Another Minneapolis observer had a different read on all this talk of record-breaking. Marion Willis Savage, owner and operator of the International Stock Food Company, was confident that if Dan did not break the record that year, his owner would put him up for sale. Savage had become convinced that Sturgis, who was more of a sportsman and gambler than a horse breeder, would, in time, be tempted to sell the horse.[7]

In fact, Savage had already discussed Dan Patch's future with Sturgis earlier in the year, and as the harness racing season wound down and the fall of 1902 encroached upon the winter, Mr. Savage approached the New Yorker with a new offer.

At Madison Square Garden on November 29, at one of the largest horse auctions of the year, the third-ranked pacer in the country, Anaconda, was sold for $7,200. Between M. W. Savage and M. E. Sturgis that price was peanuts. For three weeks the offers and counter-offers went back and forth between the two men, until Myron McHenry, who was with Dan Patch in Kansas City, headed north to Minneapolis to help close the deal between them.

On December 8, 1902, the announcement was made to the papers: Dan Patch was moving west. M. W. Savage, described by the *New York Times* as the president of "a rich corporation of the cattle and horse raising states," was the new owner of the champion pacer and had paid a jaw-dropping $60,000 for the privilege.

For weeks and months to come, horse fans in the Midwest and across the country would debate the merits of paying so much for an animal. Newspapers like the *Minneapolis Journal* analyzed the figures to see what Savage had bought himself. They estimated that Dan had won $13,800 in 1901, his only full year of racing in the stake events on the Grand Circuit. His owner at the time, Daniel Messner, had made an additional $20,000 in the sale of Dan Patch to M. E. Sturgis.

Sturgis, the paper estimated, had made about $26,000 and change over the past year through Dan's handful of races and his much longer exhibition schedule. Minus the $20,000 to Messner, and plus the $60,000 from Savage, that was a pretty good year's profit for the sportsman from New York.

If Dan Patch could continue in his impressive ways for two or three years, and if Marion W. Savage could successfully employ the stallion as the anchor of his new and mighty stock farm being built in the Minnesota River Valley, then there was a good chance Savage could realize some profit from the horse.

For M. W. Savage, however, such talk of winnings, sales prices, and the contribution Dan Patch could bring to his new stock farm didn't represent the sum of his value by a long shot. All of these would be important, but only a part of the bigger package. It is debatable whether Savage envisioned a world of Dan Patch merchandising and Dan Patch products and Dan Patch images in December 1902; but he certainly had a notion of the horse's ability as a marketing tool. Just how much value that would ultimately bring to him and his business was anybody's guess. In 1902 no one knew the value of a star athlete like Dan Patch as a marketing tool, because no one had ever used such a figure in quite the way Marion Savage was about to.

The Savage home on Portland Avenue in Minneapolis

# 5

# Mr. Savage

M. W. Savage had cherished the dream of raising high-class harness horses since childhood, but it was only in 1901, when his International Stock Food Company was making money hand over fist, that he could indulge in the luxury. Dan Patch was the most illustrious of Savage's equine purchases, but he wasn't the first. Savage had begun buying quality standardbreds a year earlier when a former world champion trotter named Directum came on the market.

With his trainer, Harry Hersey, Savage headed to a New York horse show that December and made his first foray into the world of championship harness horses by buying the twelve-year old stallion for $12,500. The arrival of Directum in Minneapolis was big news, though there were no bands or crowds to greet the old horse, who'd retired from racing half-a-dozen years earlier. A reporter visiting the trotter at the stables of M. W. Savage in the city offered a detailed description of the animal's condi-

tion and presumed state of mind: " … in his roomy boxed stall in the barn at 2600 Portland Avenue this morning [Directum] was as much at home as though he had been born and bred in Minneapolis. He was strictly on his

DIRECTUM 2:05¼

feed and was munching local oats and hay from the Minnesota bottoms with all the relish of a two-year old."

Meanwhile Savage was already formulating his idea of establishing Minnesota at the forefront of the horsebreeding world. "My reasons for buying [Directum]," he told the reporter, "were, of course, partly selfish, but on the other hand, I confess to a broad interest in the breeding of blooded horses in Minnesota. There is no finer country in the world for that purpose than this great state. All we need do is advertise that fact to the horse world and you will see the fine horse breeding industry—and a great industry it is, too—firmly established in Minnesota."[1]

A month later, Savage bought Online, another famed stallion whose racing days were long over, and he immediately began searching for property on which to stable his sires and raise the championship offspring that he envisioned would soon be trotting over the Minnesota landscape. Again, Savage's doings were noted by the press, and again he made apparent his intention of promoting the state of Minnesota to the horsebreeding world. "We have every facility for building up a race of horses here which even Kentucky can take off her hat to. We have the grass, the hay, the invigorating climate, the broad stretches of available pasturage along our river courses—in fact, everything calculated to develop to the highest perfection the most blue-blooded strain of horses."[2]

As for where the "broad stretch of pasturage" to run his own stallions would be, Savage hadn't yet made up his mind. Aside from his home and city stable on Portland Avenue, Savage owned an impressive summer cottage on Lake Minnetonka that he called Idylwild, and it was in this region, west of the city, that he first began looking for property on which to build his stock farm.

In June 1902, however, he found a large tract of land south of Minneapolis, on the rich river bottoms along the Minnesota River. There, on the south side of the river, beneath the bluffs of the town of Bloomington, Savage purchased more than 700 acres of property in a township called Hamilton and began construction on a barn and stable unlike any other in the country.

"The design, conceived by the owner, calls for a unique structure," reported a breathless writer for the *Minneapolis Journal* in August 1902. "Long sheds, in which he expects to house his constantly growing stable will radiate in the form of a wheel from a dome-shaped hub, and 'spokes' will be added as rapidly as the growth of the equine population demands. Each spoke will accommodate about thirty horses and the

The "spokes" of the International Stock Food Farm as seen from above,
with the Minnesota River in the distance to the north.

sheds will be models from every standpoint, particular attention being paid to light and ventilation. The 'hub' of the barn will be seventy feet in diameter, thus permitting construction of a 200-foot indoor track, for exercising the horses in winter or stormy weather."

The central structure, the "dome-shaped hub," was actually octagonal, and when complete it was more than ninety feet in diameter. The slightly bulbous dome was painted green, and its shape gave the stables an oriental flavor. It was actually a water tank for the horses that was fed by three nearby springs. Five capacious halls, each one 160 feet long and crowned with a string of three smaller domed cupolas, radiated out from the central structure like spokes, with enough stalls to accommodate 130 horses—and each stall had a window for ventilation.

One of the best trout streams in the region ran through the property, and a beautiful grove of 100-year old elm trees stood near the barns. There were to be cottages for the stable workers, and the Northwestern Railroad company was said to be considering a spur to the farm. Savage hired Harry Hersey as the chief trainer at the farm and then contracted Seth Griffin, the premier harness track builder of the day, to construct a mile-long track on the property.

To crown the estate and offer himself a bird's eye view of all that was happening, Savage began construction on a palatial summer home on the 125-foot bluff overlooking the farm from the north side of the river. This three-story, neo-colonial mansion was to be adorned with fluted columns, stained glass windows, and a portico made from Italian marble. It would have telephones, an elaborate intercom system, and eight acres of lawn sweeping down toward the river. When this grand home was finished, Marion Savage would be able to step outside his front door, raise a pair of binoculars to his eyes, and time the workouts taking place on the track far below him across the river without leaving his backyard.

To the plain-spoken locals who monitored the daily progress of Savage's lavish constructions, it all must have seemed pretty fabulous. Yet the best headline the Journal could come up with to announce the grandiose plan was a simple one: "Fancy Stock Farm."

Savage himself, with hardly more rhetorical flair, named his home Valley View, and the stable across the river The International Stock Food Farm.

## An Earlier Stock Farm

Though Savage's stock farm was ambitious, it was not without precedent in the area. Norman W. Kittson, the man who brought the champion pacer Johnston to the Twin Cities in 1883, had been involved in a similar enterprise just west of Saint Paul several decades earlier.

Kittson owned a line of steamboats on the Red River between Minnesota and the Dakotas, for which reason he was often referred to as "Commodore." A true pioneer of St. Paul, Kittson had begun his career before Minnesota was a state, working as a prominent agent in the Red River fur trade. (Kittson County is named after him.) In time he managed to acquire a controlling interest in a steamboat line, and he later became a partner with James J. Hill in the creation of a railroad line that eventually became the Great Northern Railroad Company.

By the time he turned his attention to harness racing, Commodore Kittson was a millionaire several times over and one of the state's wealthiest men. Over the course of the 1880s he poured large amounts of money into horse breeding and built an elaborate stable and track called Kittsondale in an area just west of St. Paul now known as the Midway district. Kittsondale had stalls for as many as ninety horses as well as a beautiful clubhouse. Above the great cooling room in the center of the stables was a sign celebrating Kittson's most famous horse: "Johnston, King of the Turf, 2:06 ¼."

Harness racing was at a peak of popularity in Minnesota at that time. Aside from Kittsondale, there were harness racing tracks in a number of southern Minnesota towns and at Minnehaha Park in Minneapolis near the famed Minnehaha waterfalls. The state fair staged a series of races every year at the track on its grounds in Hamline, and a number of other venues including Minnehaha staged races as part of the Great Western Trotting Circuit, which was a regional version of the more prestigious Grand Circuit.

During the mid-1890s, however, the economy experienced a serious cyclical downturn which affected harness racing finances in Minnesota and elsewhere in the nation. Kittsondale stopped holding races, and the track was first neglected, and later sold for industrial development. The premier track in Minneapolis at Minnehaha fell into a similar state of disrepair, and no racing events were held there between 1895 and 1901. In time the park became a popular hangout for miscreants and hoodlums—so much so that in 1904 the newly-elected mayor of Minneapolis, J. C. Haynes, pledged that "Minnehaha will be cleaned and redeemed, if it takes the whole police force of Minneapolis to do it."

The track at Kittsondale

The effort in 1901 to reestablish Great Western racing at Minnehaha was notable for the fact that it first brought Marion Willis Savage's interest in harness racing to the attention of the public. Along with "Fish" Jones, Savage was one of a handful of Minneapolis business men who arranged for a return of the Great Western Trotting circuit to the city.

## The Making of M. W. Savage

Whether Savage viewed the rise and fall of Kittsondale as a cautionary tale is doubtful. He was a forward-looking man—perhaps to a fault. According to John Hervey, "He was always so much 'on the make,' as one ambitious scheme after another unfolded before him, that he sometimes failed to realize just how things looked or sounded ... And while he was a remarkable business man, he had the failings of that class, especially in the inveteracy with which he viewed everything from the business-getting angle ... He was a man at once secretive and confidential, reserved and forthright, keeping his own counsel when he saw fit yet not disparaging that of those whom he respected."[3]

Born on an Ohio farm on March 20, 1959, Savage was raised in West Liberty, Iowa, the son of Edward W. and Rachel Savage. His father was a country doctor and pharmacist who'd served in those capacities for the Union Army during the Civil War and moved the family from Ohio to Iowa after the conflict, where M. W. Savage's one sibling, a sister, Allice, was born.

M. W.'s father took the boy on rounds with him in the countryside around West Liberty, and Savage spent time as a young man working as a clerk in a drugstore in nearby West Branch, Iowa (the birthplace of Herbert Hoover, who would have been a boy of six or seven when Marion Savage was working at the local pharmacy). According to one account, Marion's father "wished him to become a doctor and the young man commenced the study of medicine," but a love of animals, particularly a breed of horses local to eastern Iowa, called the "Bashaw," steered him toward farm life.

In 1881, M. W. Savage married a West Branch girl named Marietta Bean, and the couple moved to west central Iowa to start a livestock farm near Iowa Falls, north of Des Moines. There, in 1883, the first of two sons, Erle, was born (Harold was born 12 years later). Not long after the boy's birth the farm failed. Conflicting accounts suggest that this first enterprise was either ruined by a tornado, high water, or simply a hot, dry summer.[4]

The year before this disaster, M. W. Savage's father had died in West Branch. Precisely how his father's passing inspired Savage's next enterprise is a mystery, but after the sale of his farm in 1883 M. W. Savage opened a patent medicine business in Iowa Falls, called the Dr. E. W. Savage Medicine Company.

M. W. concocted and sold standard remedies for a variety of ailments under a "Dr. Savage's" label. These included Dr. Savage's May Apple Syrup, Dr. Savage's Stomach and Bowel Regulator, Dr. Savage's Pulmonary Balsam, Dr. Savage's Skin Remedy, Dr. Savage's Eye Water, and Dr. Savage's Blood Purifying Syrup.

It is not known whether Savage was merely continuing a business begun by his father, or using his father's name to promote a venture that he had conceived himself while working at the local pharmacy. In either case, Savage entered the patent medicine business in Iowa Falls and moved the fledgling company a short time later to Dubuque. Here he secured $25,000 in capital from local business partners and financial backers and reformed the company as the German Medicine Company. The product line—"Dr. Savage Remedies"—remained the same.

This new business quickly folded, however, with some accounts insinuating that an unscrupulous business partner undermined its financial health. Whatever the circumstances, by 1888 Savage had packed up his young family and moved north to Minneapolis, where he established another enterprise, again using the name The German Medicine Company. Here, in relatively short order, he shifted the business' focus from concocting patent medicines for humans to mixing feed supplements for animals, and he also gave his enterprise a new name: The International Stock Food Company.

In all of the marketing material published in years to come, much of which was quick to outline the successes of his business life in Minneapolis, Will Savage never detailed his background in the patent medicine business—sensitive, perhaps, to the fact that the higher circles of American society held the industry in disdain. "To the more intelligent members of the community," wrote one observer of the industry in Savage's time, "there was apparent a fraud and an exploitation of the ignorant that made the nostrum manufacturer a person whom those engaged in more proper activities did not care to meet socially."

Yet patent medicines had been a familiar part of American life since colonial times. To a large extent they merely satisfied the need for herbal medicines among urban populations that no longer had access to the appropriate herbs or the time to concoct the remedies. Patent medicines had become so popular that by the beginning of the Civil War half of all newspaper ads were devoted to them.

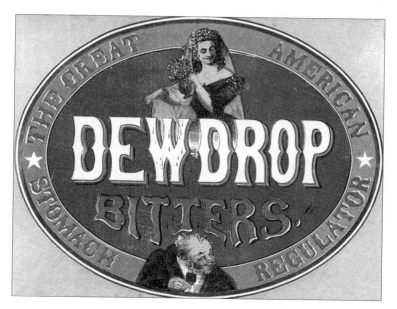

The expansion of the industry was also fueled by the circumstances of the war itself. In the 1830s the army had abolished the custom of handing its regulars a daily ration of liquor, and as a result many soldiers took to satisfying their needs with patent medicines, which were often as juiced with alcohol as any bottle of rum. The soldier's life was not an easy one: the brutality of combat, the wounds, the surgeries, the gruesome yet commonplace amputations, and the malaria, dysentery, and typhoid which were then endemic to camp life. It should surprise no one that soldiers and veterans of the Civil War self-medicated with a vengeance.

One standard remedy, Peruna, with an alcoholic content of 19 percent was so popular in the army that troops addicted to it were called "Peruna drunks." "Union supply sergeants bought Hostetter's Bitters, a brand containing 43 percent alcohol, by the case," writes Ann Anderson in *Snake Oil, Hustlers and Hambones*, a history of American patent medicines. Narcotic addiction, in general, "was so prevalent that it became known as 'the army disease.'" And with the end of the war, "many surviving combatants were inveterate self-dosers and introduced the habit to their families."

GET FAT
ON LORINGS
FAT-TEN-U
AND
CORPULA
FOODS.

The fact that many of these remedies were alcohol-based didn't seem to trouble even good temperance Christians—a population that boomed after the war (and one to which the Savage family belonged). Religious papers and journals were rife with advertising for patent medicines and teetotalers were quick to declare a distinction between the powers of medicine, which were good for you, and the powers of alcohol, which were bad. In Anderson's words, "Demon alcohol was forbidden, but a 'dose' was permissible."

In the years following the Civil War the countryside seemed to be crawling with patent medicine salesmen. Some of the products being sold door-to-door were no doubt legitimate medicines based on effective folk formulas, but many of the remedies and elixirs were little more than alcohol mixed with a random assortment of herbs, concocted by hucksters for the sole purpose of making a quick buck.

As the market for patent medicines exploded after the Civil War, so did the number of manufacturers and purveyors of medicinal products. Competition for the patent medicine dollar was fierce, and innovative advertising techniques were born in an effort to capture market share. "The Medicine Show," a staple of the last quarter of the nineteenth century, became perhaps the most popular method of selling medicinal remedies.

A turn-of-the-century patent medicine show

While there were many variations of the traveling medicine troupe, they all revolved around the mix of entertainment and salesmanship that continues to drive American show business today. Weeks before a medicine show arrived, its descent on a community would be advertised with flyers and billboards. An ostentatious parade would signal the final arrival of the now-long-anticipated company. The program itself mixed entertainment and sales pitches in proportions familiar to anyone who's ever watched an evening of network television. While there is no evidence that M. W. Savage was ever a part of the medicine show business, the techniques used to promote and stage these traveling programs would also play a part in the exhibition career of Dan Patch.

But even at the height of the era of traveling medicine shows, newspapers and the growing number of journals were probably the most important means of advertising patent medicines. Improvements in printing techniques made printing faster and typography more varied and attractive. Illustrations and contrasting typefaces made for more eye-catching ads. Promotional methods pioneered by P. T. Barnum—testimonials, hyperbole, and the use of celebrity endorsements—became commonplace for a wide array of products, including patent medicines. Whereas sheer repetition had long been the most common means of impressing a potential customer (one patent medicine company ran thirty-seven identical ads for a single product in the same newspaper issue), as the century drew to a close new technologies and marketing methods were heightening the intensity of the pitch, and those entrepreneurs who were savvy enough to develop innovative advertising techniques were the ones most likely to prosper. It was another arena in which M. W. Savage was about to shine.

# 6

# Three Feeds for One Cent

As he later described it, the idea of creating a stock food supplement business came to Savage as an inspiration and not as a permutation of the patent medicine business he was already engaged in: "Over 20 years ago," he wrote in 1905, "[I] decided that there was a large field for a High Class Medicated Stock Food to be fed to animals as an addition to their regular grain feed. This conclusion was reached because people demand salt, pepper, vinegar, mustard, etc., etc., mixed with every mouthful of their own food … I believe that it is just as essential that animals have certain Roots, Herbs, Seeds and Barks mixed with their food."[1]

Whatever might have prompted it, M. W. Savage had made a propitious decision in switching the focus of his business from patent medicines to livestock supplements and the changing world of agriculture.

Despite wheat's continued preeminence in Minnesota and elsewhere in the Upper Midwest, single crop agriculture was beginning to look less attractive to many farmers. Not only were the prices of wheat stagnant, but the risks were great for those raising a single crop in a land given to weather extremes, frequent and violent summer storms, and devastating fall and winter freezes. More farmers began to diversify, planting alfalfa, corn, oats, and barley, while also tending a greater variety of livestock. These were not subsistence operations. Profit was the goal, and as the farmers diversified, their profits rose. So, too, did production. The eggs laid in Minnesota jumped from eight million dozen in 1880 to forty-three million by 1900. Butter production increased from nineteen million pounds in 1880 to eighty-two million twenty years later.[2]

To manage these increasingly complex enterprises, individual farmers found it necessary to become their own agronomists, their own veterinarians, and their own CEOs, too, looking for any sort of edge to help them squeeze a profit out of their land and livestock year after year. To meet these needs, a new system of higher education was being developed through the land grant program at the various state universities in the Midwest, and a science of agriculture was spreading gradually through the region. All the same, isolated family farmers were seldom inclined to consult textbooks, and this opened broad avenues of ingress for entrepreneurs offering to make farm management easier and more profitable on a day-to-day basis.

M. W. Savage tailored his International Stock Food Company to fill just such a need. "After careful study and long experimenting I selected certain combination of Roots, Herbs, Barks and Seeds and decided to go into the medicated stock business. First I insisted only the highest grade of quality for every ingredient I purchased and then I could always guarantee paying results. It was a well-known fact that the average farm animal had impaired digestion and assimilation. Scientific authorities had proven time and time again that the average farm animal only digested about 55 percent of the average feed stuffs. I immediately guaranteed that 'International Stock Food' would cause animals to digest 70 to 75 percent or it would not cost the user one cent."

In other words, by adding an animal version of "salt, pepper, vinegar, etc, etc,"—a secret concoction mixed by Savage himself—farmers would be enhancing the nutritive value of their feed and the weight of their stock. If all of this sounds a little speculative, it was. Agricultural experts of the day pooh-poohed such additives, but Savage had long-since become adept at defending his products. In fact, he was a master at incorporating his ongoing battles with professors from the agricultural colleges into his sales pitch.

Like so many of the hucksters who sprang out of the age of commerce that developed in the post-Civil War United States, Savage rooted his pitch in his own unshakable confidence in the product he was selling. It was a matter of faith, primarily his own, that International Stock Food would enhance the growth and productivity of the livestock to which it was fed. But having convinced himself of the supplement's merits, he quickly began convincing others, who then sent testimonials to his offices, which Savage published with abandon.

It was a good time to be selling farm products. The golden era of family farms in the United States had arrived, and despite the slow steady movement of families into the cities, rural Americans remained the nation's most important consumers. Sears, Roebuck and Company grew to unparalleled prominence in the last years of the nineteenth century, driven by a mail order business geared expressly for rural customers. Montgomery Ward and Spiegel preceded them in the same markets, selling to all the needs of farm families from household to barnyard. The Sears line of agricultural implements alone was so extensive that in 1905 the company began publishing a separate catalog to display all the items it carried along that line.[3]

Savage rode that same wave of agricultural spending power. The International Stock Food Company experienced remarkable growth during its first ten years, largely as a result of Savage's marketing skills and the strength of the farm economy. It was not long before he began to mythologize the successes of his own company by means of a stock book catalog which gave lengthy descriptions of the products, offered testimonials to the value of his feed and medicinal products, and provided an extensive Veterinary Department describing livestock conditions and diseases from Bone Spavin to Nasal Gleet to Hog Cholera.

When International Stock Food opened its doors in 1890, it was housed in a small warehouse on Washington and Second avenues in downtown Minneapolis. There Savage and a handful of employees mixed his roots and herbs and shipped products and literature to would-be dealers and stockmen across the Midwest. Aside from its nutritive and health values, their chief claim for the additive was that it was "equally good for horses, cows and hogs." From this fact and its cost (when used in recommended doses with standard feed), Savage soon came up with a sales slogan, "3 Feeds For One Cent," which was bannered across the image of a wooden feed bucket and plastered on every piece of printed material Savage could think of.

Savage soon began adding more products to his line, mostly medicinal, like the "International Honey-Tar Foot Remedy" and "International Compound Absorbent." The business continued to grow, and in 1893 Savage moved to bigger quarters in the same area. Five years later he moved the business again, this time to a six-story building.

In 1902 he incorporated another business, The International Food Company, which produced and sold human breakfast food, along with "chemical and medicinal preparations of every kind," including washing powder, vanilla, baking powder, and "quick cleaner." Later that year, he started a biscuit company and decided to include a set of dishes as a premium for his best customers.

Advertising was at the root of Savage's business and its expansions, and he was not shy about touting just how much he spent to spread the good word about his products—in 1902 the sum exceeded $300,000. Advances in printing, including steam-powered presses and hot metal composition machines, had made the process more economical, and by the turn of the century Savage had established his own lithography department at International Stock Food, where he became a pioneer in the process of turning out colored-print advertising. These images became a staple of his catalog stock books and were also distributed in the form of prints, which were sent to dealers all across the country to give away to customers. The pictures, which would soon feature Dan Patch and other famed harness horses in the International Stock Farm stable, could be seen hanging on farmhouse walls throughout the country. Savage would later incorporate his own publishing company, Earth Publishing, and place it under the management of two long-time associates, his brother-in-law, E. H. Forster, and Charles Veeder.

As his many enterprises continued to flourish, Savage began to devote increasing space in his catalogue to the story of own his life and legend as a businessman—told by M. W. Savage. He would describe the growth of his company and its moves from one imposing warehouse to the next in downtown Minneapolis. He would tell how much he was able to spend on advertising, how many people he employed, and how many people bought his products world-wide. He published photos of his beautiful new city home on Portland Avenue in Minneapolis, and photos of Idylwild, his gay summer home on Lake Minnetonka. In time, he would also tell the tale of how he came to purchase Dan Patch. It was his own personal Horatio Alger story, punctuated by advertisements for remedies for nasal gleet and hog splavin.

It was a wild ride of expansion for Savage, and any bumps in the road of success were quickly smoothed. He was a master at turning his own quarrels into grist for his advertising. For example, details of the company's ongoing spats with the agricultural departments of certain unnamed agricultural colleges in the Midwest became a standard feature of the International Stock Food catalog. Savage would stand four-square for the honesty of his advertising, and rail against "the Political Salary Suckers" working at "some of our agricultural colleges." According to accounts from the catalog, agricultural bulletins published by these universities warned farmers against the high cost of using the stock food supplement as a feed. But his product wasn't a feed, Savage would say, time-and-again in his catalog. It was a feed supplement. "The Label states plainly that it is a medicinal preparation. All of our advertising states that it is a medicinal preparation, and that a feeder cannot afford to use it on any other basis."

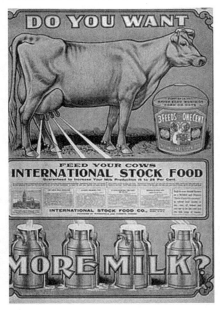

In 1898, Savage took the tactic to a new level. During the Spanish-American War, the federal government slapped a tax on all medicinal products shipped to the war effort. No such levy was assigned to stock feed going to Cuba or the Philippines. To confirm his assertion that his International Stock Feed was not a livestock food, but a medicinal supplement, and against the suggestion of the agency itself, Savage insisted to the U.S. Internal Revenue that he be taxed for shipping goods to the effort. With just the sort of tone Savage was hoping for, the *Minneapolis Journal* reported the story with head-shaking admiration:

"He and some two other manufacturers of stock foods prefer to pay the government thousands of dollars in taxes rather than do what their competitors are doing—that is evade the law with the approval of the revenue officials."

The total bill for his obstinacy would come to $40,000. But the anecdote with its accompanying sum would be told over and over in the International Stock Food catalog for years to come as further testimony to M. W. Savage's forthright and honest nature.

## The Expo Building

By the time Dan Patch arrived in Minneapolis, the International Stock Food Company was the largest stock food company in the world, worth over a million dollars. It employed 300 people, 130 of whom did office work. The company received and responded to half a million letters annually. It was so short of space that it strung typewriters from the ceiling to be raised and lowered as necessary throughout the day.

To accommodate his ever-expanding need for space, Savage made another grand purchase in April 1903, just five months after buying Dan Patch. He acquired the famed Minneapolis Exposition Building in downtown Minneapolis, across the river from the Union Depot. The new quarters provided 750,000 square feet of work space for his employees, making it the largest plant in the city of Minneapolis.

The Expo Building had been constructed fifteen years earlier as a municipal drawing card for trade shows and fairs. It quickly reached the height of its fame when the National Republican Party held its convention there in 1892 but subsequently fell into disrepair and neglect with equal rapidity—so much so, in fact, that when Savage purchased the property he was hailed for his civic-mindedness.

The new building covered a full city block and provided eighteen acres of floor space for Savage's continually expanding enterprises. It was located on the east side of the river just above St. Anthony Falls and when renovations were completed would feature what Savage claimed was the world's largest single-room office. Located on the second floor

The Expo Building

above the central hall where the nation's Republican leaders had done their nominating and speechifying nearly a dozen years earlier, this room, 125 feet wide and 525 feet long, would soon house the mammoth typewriting department of the International Stock Food Company, with typewriters now resting permanently on their desktops.

In the spirit of civic improvement, Savage promised to keep the main-floor hall open and available to horse, stock, and automobile shows. He also vowed to improve nearby riverfront property and turn it into a public park, "if the civic authorities will elevate the moral tone of the neighborhood." Main Street, to the southeast of the Exposition building, was at that time said to be monopolized by houses of ill repute.[4]

It had been a remarkable run for M. W. Savage. He had moved his business into the largest plant in Minneapolis, brought the renowned pacer Dan Patch to Minneapolis, and begun the construction of his International Stock Food Farm south of the Minnesota River—all within the space of a year. These events thrust Savage onto the public stage in Minnesota in a way few business leaders in the region had

The main office, laboratory, and labeling department at the new plant

previously experienced. In just fifteen years, this obscure young patent medicine salesman from Iowa had turned an idea for a feed supplement business into an industry giant. He'd made perhaps the most high-profile purchase in the history of the city, while at the same time winning the hearts and minds of the community by suggesting that his main purpose in bringing Dan Patch to Minnesota was to jump-start a horse-breeding industry. He'd further solidified his standing in Minneapolis by buying one of its landmark downtown buildings and filling it with his thriving business.

In 1903 Savage was only forty-four years old. As he stood in the backyard of his magnificent, newly-constructed home on the bluffs above the Minnesota River, looking down on the fancy stock farm he'd built and scrutinizing the workouts of his greatest purchase, M. W. Savage must have had the distinct impression that the world was his oyster.

M. W. Savage and son Erle looking south from Valley View toward the stock farm

# 7

# Against the Clock

Dan Patch was doing pretty well for himself, too. He spent a frolicking spring in plush new quarters on the Minnesota River, luxuriating in the river bottom grasses and at The Taj, where he trained on the mile track before the watchful eyes of M. W. Savage, Harry Hersey, and all those who cared to make the ten-mile journey out Lyndale Avenue from Minneapolis to the countryside.

That spring of 1903 Dan began work as a sire for Savage, helping his new boss bolster both the racing stock of the state of Minnesota and any horse breeder willing to ship his mares to the International Stock Food Farm. The pages of Savage's stock books would soon carry advertisements for his studs, with pictures of Dan Patch as the Calendar Boy: "Breed Your Good Mare to one of my Stallions and you will surely raise a very high Class Colt, that might develop into a World Champion worth $25,000 to $50,000. You may be the lucky man who will produce a champion." The fee for a session with Dan Patch was set at $300.[1]

The farm became a destination spot for all who were curious to see the magnificent stables and their prized horses. In mid-March, the Omaha Road railway company decided to designate the stop at Savage's farm as the Savage station rather than Hamilton. The U.S. Post Office soon followed suit, when M. W. Savage began using the farm as a mailing address for his burgeoning stock business, and in 1904 the township officially adopted the name Savage.

All of this busy-ness at the farm worried Myron McHenry, who tended to believe Dan's energies were being stretched too thin by all of the attention, particularly that conjugal work. (He was bred to about twenty mares that first spring according to one source.) During this honeymoon period of his relationship with Savage, McHenry held his tongue, but there would be conflicts to come over how Dan Patch should and shouldn't be used. From McHenry's perspective, Dan's primary role was as champion pacer of the nation, and he should be trained as such. The horse's stud work was physically depleting and should be kept to a minimum.

In April the *New York Times* speculated on the prospect of a series of summer races between Dan Patch and Prince Alert, but no one in Dan's camp was fueling the talk. As Savage had stated the moment Dan arrived in Minneapolis, the pacer was not going to be racing horses any time soon. His only opponent, for the foreseeable future, would be the clock, against which he would run in a series of exhibitions to be scheduled for the summer and fall of 1903.

There was risk involved in this decision, however. Despite the tradition of timed exhibitions in harness racing, the competitive drama of horses racing one against another was part of the excitement of seeing a champion. Savage was gambling that it would be possible to fill grandstands with crowds who wanted to see Dan Patch race against his own best times. As much as Dan Patch was the beau ideal of a pacer for the horse-racing public, it could be a pretty disappointing day at the track to see an exhibition that didn't set or at least approach a record-setting pace, and even a horse like Dan would have a hard time drawing crowds after a few less-than-sterling performances.

On the other hand, as he was about to prove, no one was more adept than Will Savage at getting the crowds out. Through his thousands of International Stock Food Company dealers and his advertising machinery in Minneapolis, he had the mechanisms in place to spread the word about Dan Patch exhibitions anywhere the horse might appear. Dan's lineage and race history had already made him a good "stud" upon which to build a stock farm. He could also be a solid "spokesman" for the International Stock Food Company for years to come simply on the strength of his record; yet M. W. Savage wanted more from his horse than to be a tool of advertising and a great sire.

In January, he'd suggested that Dan was capable of 1:57, which was setting the bar to a mark higher than any other harness horse, pacer, or trotter had ever risen. In fact, it had taken harness horses most of the nineteenth century to crack the two-minute mile. A long string of great horses, including John R. Gentry, Robert J, and Dan's own sire Joe Patchen, had failed to break the barrier. It was not until 1897 that a single pacer, Star Pointer, had done it. That Star Pointer's time had not been repeated until Dan Patch himself broke the two-minute mark in 1902 was some indication of the challenge. For Savage to suggest that Dan could drop a full two seconds off the record pace was nothing short of audacious. It represented both a challenge to his own horse and an invitation to harness racing fans across the country: If you want to see my horse fall on his face, Marion Savage was saying, or if you want to see him break a new mark, come out to the track.

Either way was money in the bank for Savage.

## Brighton Beach

"Dan Patch, the champion pacer, who is now at the International Stock Food Farm on the Minnesota River, will be shipped within the next fortnight to Cleveland, where his driver, Myron McHenry, will prepare him for his campaign against time around the grand circuit this summer," the *Minneapolis Journal* announced in May 1903. "The tentative program arranged by M. W. Savage, owner of Dan Patch, and McHenry, contemplates a tour of the southern cities, followed by exhibition miles on the principal tracks in the East. In the fall, Dan Patch will be brought west, and will go against time in Minneapolis."[2]

McHenry headed to Cleveland ahead of the horse and continued to hype the coming season. The horse had had a good winter and spring in Minnesota, he said, and he hinted that even the earliest viewers of Dan Patch that season would be seeing something special. "I will not have to put in weeks and months, as some trainers have to do ... I will have a strong well-muscled horse when he reaches me."

The horse was as good as McHenry's word. After a few weeks of training in Ohio, the season began, not in Cleveland but Columbus, where Dan Patch ran an exhibition half-mile in :57 ¾ seconds. Three weeks later, he was in Erie, Pennsylvania, racing on a half-mile track, where he bested the track record of 2:10 ¼ for a mile-run by doing his two laps in 2:09. The next week, at the track in Yonkers, New York, before a large crowd, Dan whipped around a very loose track in high wind in a time of 2:00 ¼ , not enough to beat the 1:59 ¼ mark, but a good portent for the racing season.

Back at Brighton Beach in Brooklyn for the third time in his career, just a week after his appearance in Yonkers, Dan was greeted royally by the crowd. He had apparently captured the hearts of the tough New York audience.

The front page of the *New York Times* the next day told the story: "A new world's harness race record of 1:59 was established at the Brighton Beach race track yesterday when in a race against time Dan Patch, the fastest harness horse in the world, and the unbeaten pacing champion, astonished patrons of the turf by overcoming a combination of unfavorable conditions, and covering a mile in time a quarter of a second faster than the distance ever was covered by a harness horse before."

The adverse conditions included a wet track and a stiff ocean breeze, which had made a record run doubtful. Even so, McHenry brought Dan up from the stables near the appointed hour of four o'clock, accompanied by two pacing horses: the first, who would race alongside Dan as "a galloper," was driven by "Doc" Tanner, a noted horseman on the circuit; a second runner followed behind, driving Dan from the rear.

Exhibition races, like harness races in general, began on the fly, with the driver, after warming up his horse on the track, giving a signal to the starters that he was ready to go as he and the horse neared the start wire. So it was with McHenry and Dan Patch that day at Brighton Beach. As he drove Dan Patch toward the grandstand, McHenry nodded to the judges and the word for the start was given with Dan Patch in full stride. The official timers started their watches as he passed the judges' stand, close on the rail and already going at top speed. The *Times* later reported that Dan continued hugging the inside through the first turn "so close to the pole that his sulky wheel almost grazed the fence."

Dan did the first quarter in :29 ½, and the half in a speed-burning :58 ½. The crowd, hearing the announced time and sensing a record in the making, sent up a prolonged cheer. But in the third quarter, Dan hit the ocean breeze full in the face, and his pace for the quarter dropped markedly to 1:29 ¼.

It was at this point that Tanner, driving the galloper, pulled ahead of Dan Patch, helping to cut the wind. Almost immediately, Dan returned to the same even pace and power of stroke that he'd displayed earlier in the race, and he finished the mile in 1:59, a quarter of a second better than the old mark, thus cementing his place of honor as the fastest horse in the world of harness racing.

There was a little grumbling after the race about the use of "Doc" Tanner and his runner as a windbreak, but that peccadillo would be eclipsed soon enough by other far more egregious examples of bending the rules during a timed exhibition. Marion Willis Savage happily pocketed the $2,500 check offered by the Brighton Beach Track Association for the record, and most horsemen in New York were satisfied that they had, in fact, just witnessed a genuine record time produced by the best pacer in the country.

Just four trials into the season, Dan Patch had already surpassed his record-breaking time from a year earlier, and there were still eleven engagements to come. Whether this would be the high-water mark of Dan Patch's year or merely the beginning of a repeatedly phenomenal season was anybody's guess, but most expected even better times out of the horse.

The *Chicago Tribune* was frankly astonished by the abilities of the horse. It used its editorial page two days after the Brighton Beach exhibition to extol the virtues of the pacer under a headline that read simply, "Dan Patch, Champion":

> *That quarter of a second which Dan Patch knocked off his record day before yesterday had a distinct money meaning. It made him a more valuable commodity than he ever was before. But let us forget that he is a commodity. Let us remember only that he is the most magnificent and the most magnanimous horse that ever put on harness. May he live long and prosper.*

But in other quarters, it was all beginning to seem like old hat for Dan Patch. As he headed home from New York to race for the first time in his new home state of Minnesota, "Fish" Jones implied that the pacer's achievements were simply to be expected from such a great horse: "Dan Patch's peerless performances at Brighton Beach did not electrify the world as has been the custom of occurrences of record breaking in the past," he wrote in his journal, The *Northwestern Horseman and Stockman*. "The press and public were well prepared for Dan's delivery of a new target for harness horses."

Racetrack infield at the Minnesota State Fair, ca. 1905

# 8

# "Our State Fair is a Great State Fair"

At the turn of the twentieth century, the United States was already transforming itself from a rural to an urban society, but at that moment, perhaps more than any other, its population fell into two more or less equal nations. Even as urban areas swelled with new immigrants and industries, a thriving rural economy continued to support countless small communities across the country.

State fairs thrived in this balance. Here the worlds of the city and the country were joined each year in lengthy, ritualized celebrations, which brought huge numbers of consumers to the city and informed rural folks about the latest in technology and popular culture.

By 1903 no state fair in the union was more popular or successful than Minnesota's. Set on permanent fair grounds in the township of Hamline, midway between the Twin Cities of Minneapolis and Saint Paul, the Minnesota State Fair topped its nearest competitors, Illinois and Iowa, in the numbers of exhibitors it included, the elegance and refinement of the grounds and buildings, and the revenues it generated.[1]

The fair was first and foremost a place of commerce. Farmers strengthened their herds and scrutinized the latest in machinery, while their wives inspected the butter-making equipment and gathered new ideas about household management at the brand new Agricultural Building. Vast acres of the grounds were devoted to farming implements, and visitors lined up to see prize-winning cows, horses, pigs, and poultry in the freshly-painted stock barns. There was a horticultural exhibition as well, and livestock shows and parades were scheduled throughout the week.

Modern gas lines serviced the restaurants scattered across the fairgrounds and also the brand-new Manufacturer's Building. For sports enthusiasts there was bicycle racing and track and field events. A women's building staffed with volunteers from the Federated Women's Clubs of Minnesota promoted the latest interests of the clubs, which included in 1903 the preservation of Minnesota's rapidly disappearing white pine forests and the beautification of the state's urban areas.

Meanwhile, rural bumpkins spied city slickers on the Midway, or Pike, as it was more commonly called, and these "pikers" each became a little less distanced by the glance. To make sure these gatherings were conducted with sobriety, the state had banned the sale of alcohol within a mile of the fairgrounds, though a thirsty visitor could find more than one Blind Pig in the township of Hamline, and more than a few pockets on the fairgrounds held flasks of good-for-what-ailed-ya.

Two rail lines, one from Minneapolis and one from Saint Paul, led directly into the heart of the fairgrounds at Hamline, depositing visitors in the middle of the fair, within two hundred yards of the grandstand. Exhibition barns were to the west; the Agricultural Building was to the east. As the fairgoers departed the train, they would be standing smack-dab in front of the arched entrance to the Pike, modeled after the one built for the upcoming Saint Louis Exposition. A ten-cent entrance fee "would provide much to see without any further cost," though most of the numerous sideshows within cost an additional dime, and some of them were even a quarter!

The Midway at the Minnesota State Fair, ca 1905

Just inside the main entrance of the Pike, Youturkey the Japanese Marvel worked the high wire from a height of 100 feet. Beside him, also doing acrobatics in their first North American engagement (or so the advertisements claimed) was the Picheen family from Chile. Then came the gymnastic Brothers Steiner doing somersaults from a twenty-five foot ladder and Big Abdullah the Arabian Chieftan, who employed eleven acrobats and one lion tamer, who almost invariably stopped the show by performing something called a "skirt dance" and then placing her head into the mouth of the largest lion.

Elsewhere on the pike there was a dog, monkey, and pony show "especially arranged for ladies and children," a Crystal Maze, a Laughing Parlor, Topsey-Turvey Land, The Palace of Mysteries, The Glass Palace, The Hall of Illusions, The Cave of Winds, The Electric Theater, and mysteriously, Roberta in Poses.

The Fair would end each evening with a pyrotechnic spectacular. In 1903 the Burning of Rome was re-created on a site that spanned several acres of the grounds and featured an elaborate model of the city constructed for just this occasion (in other years, equally dramatic and destructive scenes from ancient and modern history would be staged— Vesuvius erupting one year, the destruction of Port Arthur from the Sino-Japanese War of 1904 the next). The show would last for two hours and feature scenes of ancient Rome, complete with actors and extras, all leading up to the infamous fire and the despicable moment when Nero grabs his fiddle. For the average Minnesotan at the turn of the twentieth century, urban or rural, this was jaw-dropping stuff.

Newspapers in the Twin Cities were genuinely concerned about the effects of all of this head-turning entertainment on the country folk. Before the 1904 fair, the *Minneapolis Daily News* sent reporter Kent Holen on an undercover assignment to a station northwest of the cities because "every year during fair week the newspapers are filled with accounts of all sorts of confidence games whereby country visitors are buncoed out of their money." Holen was dispatched to uncover to what extent the allegations were true.

Disguised as "Ben Johnson, farmer," Holen climbed aboard a train bound for the State Fair. He headed straight for the smoking car and soon found himself seated next to a man in a black suit, derby hat, and glasses, who, as he later put it, "turned out to be one of the smoothest grifters I ever met." The man claimed he was Dr. Boeckman of St. Paul, an oculist, selling glasses. In a few minutes, he had his valise open and "Ben Johnson" was trying on a variety of spectacles, including a pair with gold rims made for a customer in Alexandria who no longer wanted them. "Dr. Boeckman" offered to sell Farmer Johnson these glasses at the low, low price of $7.50. For an extra three dollars, he would charge the glasses with electricity, which "would not only make them stronger permanently but also prevent them from steaming."

Holen played along with all of this, waiting to spring his secret identity on the unsuspecting scammer and get a reaction for his readers. Unfortunately for Holen, in the midst of the sales job, Dr. Boeckman pulled out a wad of two-dollar bills and asked several in the car if they could change his roll for a twenty. It turned out that Holen just happened to have one of those in his pocket. He swapped his bill for what he thought was a roll of ten $2 bills, and then went back to bargaining over the glasses. It turned out that the roll of two's was, in fact, a mix of one's and two's.

"I hate to admit it," he told his readers the next day, "but it all happened so naturally and was so far removed from the spectacle bunco that I walked right into the trap. I changed a $20 bill and lost $5 on the deal."[2]

## But No Gambling

For all its apparent worldliness, gambling was illegal at the state fairgrounds, and only harness racing, not thoroughbred, was on the schedule. The state of Minnesota had banned gambling at the track in 1895 and a bill in the 1903 legislative session to encourage the breeding of thoroughbreds and regulate "race meetings"—a back-door means, said its opponents, to enable gambling in the state—had gotten nowhere fast. One of the measure's leading opponents was none other than Will Savage, who smelled a rat in the legislation and said so in a letter to the *Minneapolis Journal*: "The 'thoroughbred' horse is a certain breed of horse which is used almost exclusively in this country for running races where pools are sold ... Since gambling on horse races has been abolished in our state," Savage said, "there has been a better class of people evincing an interest in horse racing at our fair, and the attendance has been much larger."

Savage, who had so often trumpeted his intentions of boosting the horsebreeding business in Minnesota, was not in the least interested in promoting the raising of thoroughbreds and made no apologies for any inconsistencies in his thinking. "Minnesota does not raise horses of this breed and never will to any extent, and a bill to encourage the breeding of 'thoroughbred' horses is too ridiculous for serious consideration."

To his mind, and the mind of many other harness racing fans across the country, thoroughbred racing was trouble, pure and simple. It was a mind-set captured nicely by Meredith Wilson, some fifty years later in *The Music Man*, when Professor Harold Hill warns the River

City youth about the dangers of thoroughbred gambling. Trouble, with a capital T, began when "out of town jaspers" arrived to promote horse racing: "Not a wholesome trotting race, no, but a race where they set right down on the horse! Like to see some stuck-up jockey boy sittin' on Dan Patch?"

## Dan Patch at His First Fair

Dan Patch and his entourage were just wholesome enough to fit into the state fair milieu like a hand in a glove. A little bit urban and a little bit rural, Dan lured both "the sharps" and "the flats" into the fairground at Hamline. Will Savage understood this basic appeal, and for weeks prior to Dan's first appearance at the Minnesota State Fair the advertising department at the International Stock Food Company was cranked into full gear. In a pattern that was still developing but would be perfected through the course of Dan's racing career, both the urban papers and the rural sheets for miles around started to print pictures and stories featuring Dan. Advertising wagons owned and operated by Savage scoured the countryside plastering every available billboard, building, and fence with huge posters that not only announced the upcoming appearance of Dan Patch and his troupe at the fair, but also underscored the merits of Savage's 'three feeds for a cent' International Stock Food. "Your Chance of a Lifetime," said the papers. "The Only Appearance of Dan Patch in the Northwest this Season." All across the state, from Winona to Pipestone and from Stillwater to Elk River, the word got around that Dan's appearance at the state fair was one thing not to be missed. [3]

The hype aside, genuine interest in witnessing a world-class event was both widespread and deep-rooted. One reporter for the *Minneapolis Tribune* wrote: "By far the greatest track event ever seen in the West will be the attempt of Dan Patch to lower his own world's record at the Minnesota State Fair Grounds on Monday, August 31, the opening day of the coming fair."

Dan was scheduled to run three times, it was reported. "First, will be a good warming-up heat, after a while will come one which will be pretty near the record, then, finally when the pacer is in the finest trim, McHenry will let him go for the new mark. What that will be remains to be seen."[4]

Will Savage had asked for a flat fee of the State Fair Board for Dan's appearance, but the committee had balked at the price of $2,000, preferring to offer him a percentage of the day's gate instead. He agreed to the stipulations, which included a proviso that if "admissions and grand stand tickets did not exceed those of last year the owner was to have nothing." On the other hand, if they did surpass last year's mark, Savage and Dan would get 80 percent of the increase up to $3,250 and 50 percent of anything above that.[5]

The opening day of the fair, when Dan was set to race, was traditionally the least attended of the week-long event, which may have prompted the State Board's negotiating strategy. But any backslapping among members in the wake of their deal with Will Savage ceased when the turnstiles started clicking. First day attendance for the 1903 fair was 42,000, an increase of 17,000 from the previous year. And as much as the fairgoers may have appreciated the speech given by Indiana Senator Charles Fairbanks during the opening ceremonies, that jump wasn't on his account.

Dan Patch and Will Savage would earn more than $5,500 on the basis of their complicated and seemingly risky deal. And in years to come, Will Savage would routinely negotiate similar arrangements for exhibitions at fairgrounds across the country, and routinely make a killing in the process. Savage was frequently lauded for his acumen in insisting upon a percentage of the gate rather than a flat fee, but it appears as if it was the Minnesota State Fair Board which first suggested such a deal. It wasn't the last time the board would end up with egg on its face in its dealing with W. M. Savage.

## The First Run

Senator Fairbanks delivered his speech to open the fair at about noon that day to a grandstand crown of more than 5,000. The topic was modern agriculture. "Farming is more and more coming to be a scientific pursuit," he said. "Methods which were unknown to our fathers are continually and rapidly taking the place of the old."

Fairbanks predicted that all of this modernity in farm life would boost the future health of the rural life. "The tendency to gravitate to the city will in good time be followed by a return drift to the country. Improved methods in farming, increased comforts of farm life, which come through experience and systematic education will be the magnets which will draw from the congregated centers to the agricultural communities."[6]

Fairbanks was obviously not a great prognosticator. Nor was he the chief attraction that day. It was to the magnetic Dan Patch that the citizens of both the congregated centers and the agricultural communities were drawn. From the fairgrounds into the arena streamed the good folks of Minnesota, wearing straw boaters and flowered hats to guard against the late August sun.

The grandstand at the Minnesota State Fair was a double-decker affair built with its back to the rest of the grounds on the south side of the mile-long oval track. Twenty thousand men and women crowded into the seats for Dan's afternoon run, with another eight thousand blanketing Machinery Hill to the east of the oval. The track infield also housed clusters of spectators watching the horses. Beyond them to the north could be seen a cornfield, turning golden in the afternoon heat.

The crowd in the grandstands had been dividing its attention between some preliminary pacing heats on the oval and the performance of Calvert, a tight-rope performer. It was after 3 o'clock when a cheer suddenly went up from the far end of the stand and then the cry, "Dan Patch!"

From the stables trotted the mahogany-colored stallion. "Necks were craned, and men and women climbed onto their seats to see the great horse as he moved like a smooth-running machine down the track and by the grand stands ... now and then he proudly turned his handsome head and reviewed his admirers."

McHenry drove Dan on a few short warm-up runs, even as the pacers already occupying the track continued with their races. "In driving up the stretch Patch passed the 2:40 class, making for the wire, but showing no regard for his inferiors, he moved on by them without notice and continued his easy gait around the circuit."

When the heat finished and the 2:40 horses and their drivers left the track, another horse and sulky appeared and started warming up. The crowd quickly understood that this was Dan's "runner," the pace horse, who would try to push the champion to a record time. Suddenly, with no announcement, Dan and his racing partner passed beneath the start wire and were away like the wind.

Stopwatches clicked all around the grandstand, marking the first quarter-mile and then the half. There was a murmur of disappointment in the stands as the times showed Dan to be well off a record pace. The more knowledgeable viewers in the stands quickly let track newcomers know that this wasn't the run. It was all still warming up. At the end of the jog McHenry, speaking through a megaphone, confirmed for the crowd that Dan was just easing in to his exhibition—a go at the record was still to come. The horse was lead off to the stables, having just completed a 2:10 mile, and the crowds nursed their not-yet-vanquished hopes of witnessing history.

During the interim there was more entertainment from the tightrope artist. Here and there spectators could be seen nipping discretely from well-concealed hip flasks, and more than a few enthusiasts placed wagers with their friends, based on the horse's first run and the condition of the track, as to whether Dan Patch would be able to top the 1:59 he had posted at Brighton Beach. Half an hour later Dan Patch was back on the track and McElroy once again put his megaphone to use, announcing, as the newspaper put it "that the time had at last arrived and the spectators were now to see the champion pacer of the world try for a new record."

The runner joined Dan back out on the track and after a short drive the two horses approached the start wire and were suddenly off, the runner in the lead and Dan straining to catch him. But something was wrong and McHenry quickly pulled up. He was not satisfied with the start, and a bell clanged, the horses were slowed, and, once again, the crowd took a deep breath as Dan and the runner turned back.

Thirty thousand pulses quickened and slowed. But after a few more minutes on the track, Dan Patch and the runner were aimed once again toward their running start beneath the wire. This time McHenry nodded as his horse neared the wire. Stopwatches clicked and the crowd roared as the two horses sped by.

Tucked into his sulky, and with his legs stretched on either side of Dan Patch's rear haunches, McHenry held his whip upright in his right hand through the first quarter mile, which passed in thirty breathless seconds. Beneath the crowd on Machinery Hill the horses were even, Dan flying gracefully in the side-to-side rock of the pacer as his partner galloped on.

Just before the half-mile mark, on the far side of the track, Dan passed the runner, and observant viewers could see McHenry giving his driving mate a nod soon after, asking for more speed from the pace horse. At the half, a glance at the watch showed :59 ¾.

The driver of the speed horse gave his steed the whip and pulled even at the three-quarters pole, and then eased out ahead. Dan continued to keep his pace but needed to best a thirty-second last quarter to break his own world record. The crowd could see the beauty of him at the last turn, straining with the graceful effort of a great athlete as he came down the straightaway toward the grandstand. The question was, would that lovely gait be enough to help him top 1:59?

At the wire, just beneath the wildly cheering crowd in the grandstand, Dan Patch finally pulled even with the runner, and it was easy to see why fans could forget they were watching a timed exhibition and not a race. The yells and huzzahs echoed for a moment on the grounds, but then the farmers and merchants, the mechanics and field hands, went eerily silent as the horses eased into a slow trot. All eyes shifted toward the timeboard near the judge's box at the foot of the grandstands, waiting for the posting. Did he beat it? Had they just seen a record run?

Those who held their own stopwatches already had a clue, but they shook their heads and waited for an official posting. When the numbers went up on the board—a 2:00— brief moment of disappointment came and went.

There were certainly grousers in the stands that day who found fault with the way McHenry drove and criticized Savage for shipping the horse cross-country and then expecting him to perform in record time, but most of the spectators were well aware that they'd seen something special. The best pacer in the country had just sped around the track of the Minnesota State Fair right before their very eyes. They were cheering for both the horse and themselves. Not only had Dan Patch shaved more than five seconds off the best harness-racing time previously recorded in the state of Minnesota, but they had been there to see it. The Minnesota State Fair was suddenly the place to be for an American harness racing fan, and the state's sons and daughters shouted their approval and appreciation to McHenry, Will Savage, and most especially, to that dark brown stallion.

As Dan Patch clip-clopped back to the judge's stand beneath the assembly and received the traditional floral horseshoe from W. B.

MacLean, president of the Lake of the Isles Driving Club, he heard a rousing series of ovations.

In a button-popping speech, which nonetheless represented the general sentiment of the audience, MacLean said, "The people of this state, especially those interested in the introduction and breeding of fine horses can never over-estimate the good which has been done by Mr. Savage to this section of the country. The greatest horse in the world is owned in Minnesota by one of Minneapolis's leading businessmen. It is indeed something of which every Minnesotan should be proud."[7]

Young Harold Savage driving Dan Patch

# 9

# "Good Enough For A Buggy Horse"

From the Minnesota State Fair, Dan Patch traveled to Lima, Ohio, where he did a 2:04 mile on a half-mile track. Then it was on to Hartford, Connecticut on September 10, where he raced a 2:01 exhibition, and then north to Readville, Massachusetts, where Dan paced the mile in 2 minutes flat. In less than three weeks, he'd traveled more than 3000 miles and raced four times, an exhausting schedule, and there was much more to come that fall of 1903.

The whirlwind pace didn't sit well with at least one important member of the Dan Patch team—Myron McHenry. McHenry had groused during the spring about Dan's stud sessions, and now he complained about Dan's grueling schedule. Track wags, however, whispered that Savage had complaints of his own about McHenry and his lifestyle—in particular, the trainer's drinking habits.

All of this would be settled in due time, but in September there was still much racing to do, and a more public controversy was brewing. On the twenty-third, just as Dan was finishing yet another exhibition in Ohio (where he'd once again cracked the two-minute mile by pacing at 1:59 ½), word came from the Empire Track in Yonkers, New York, that Prince Direct had just shattered Dan Patch's record by racing a 1:57 mile. Following the landmark effort, Prince Direct's owners had issued a challenge to Dan and Will Savage to quit the solo exhibitions and face Prince in a match race to see who was the better horse.

In the minds of many racing fans, however, Prince Direct's record was suspect. Taking a cue from bicycle racers who'd often ridden behind a variety of windbreaks, including automobiles—and, in one memorable exhibition, a Long Island Train—Prince Direct had made his Yonkers record behind a large canvas shield. The wedge-shaped cloth was carried by a pacemaker racing directly ahead of the Prince, who tucked in behind it and sailed over the mile like a clipper ship. While horsemen tended to forgive Dan Patch for his use of a pacesetter, they were far less indulgent toward the artificial windbreak exploited by Prince Direct during his record-breaking run. It was widely felt that limits needed to be put in place on such time trials. What Prince Direct had done was sneered at by one writer as "wind-resistance driving pushed to the point of eccentricity" and described as "Auto-trotto-yachtic" racing by an inventive writer for The *New York Sun*.[1]

It wasn't Prince Direct's only unfair advantage, either, according to critics. Prince raced wearing hopples, the leg harnesses used to ensure that a pacer didn't break his gait. The device would soon be commonly used by pacers, but it was still new to the world of harness racing in 1903 and was employed at the time primarily to help train young pacers who were prone to break their gait. To use them in a timed exhibition or a race was seen by purists as a cheat. A horse's gait should strictly be a product of heredity and training, these critics said. "In such devices as hopples they saw only a tricky and vicious interference with [a horse's] natural way of going. It admitted to the racing events horses that, left to themselves, bungled their work."[2]

There was a final damning accusation. According to track writer Henry Ten Eyck White of the *Chicago Tribune*, "Besides wearing the hopples, without the aid of which [Prince Direct] cannot strike a gait that would keep a street car busy, the Prince is known as a 'hop horse.'" Just what sort of "hop," or stimulant, Prince Direct might have been taking was never verified, but M. W. Savage stated publicly that some of the horse's best miles "have been passed with a jorum of coffee and whiskey taken just before the start."

While the accusation was never verified, Savage refused to let his horse face a challenger whom he considered to be sullied. "Prince Alert has never paced a mile even in two minutes under natural conditions," Savage told the *Minneapolis Journal* the day after Prince Alert's record-setting run, "and it is generally believed that hoppled and 'stimulated' he cannot beat two minutes without a high wind shield that will completely protect him from the natural air resistance."[3]

Savage also appealed directly to the U.S. Trotting Association, the body that oversaw harness racing records-keeping. "I want to go on record as opposed to freak or mechanical records for trotters or pacer. Leave the horse to meet the air resistance just as he meets it in a race or in a matinee on the road," he told the *Journal* reporter. "I certainly believe these gentlemen of the association will decide in favor of the horse under everyday, natural conditions, and by so doing greatly advance the legitimate horse interests."

In the end, the Trotting Association would take Savage's advice: Prince Direct's record would not be acknowledged. But this was not to be the last word from the association on pacing records, and Will Savage would not always be so pleased with that body's rulings.

## The True Value of Dan Patch

There was one other September distraction for Will Savage.

In the spring of 2003, just four months after he purchased the stallion, M. W. Savage had entertained the first of many offers for Dan—$70,000, he told the *Minneapolis Journal,* without revealing the source of the offer, a $10,000 bump in the horse's value, though he'd yet to appear in a race. He turned down another chance to sell Dan Patch in August for $65,000.

When the time came in September to assess Dan Patch's value for tax purposes, however, Savage incurred a few quizzical notices from both the public and the tax assessors by valuing his prize-winning pacer at $261—the same figure he applied to all his horses at the stable at the International Stock Farm.

The Hennepin County board of assessment would have none of it. They set the value of Savage's full stable at $30,000, a figure that dropped the jaw of more than a few Minneapolis horse owners. MacLean, the president of the Lake of the Isles Driving Club, who had just presented Dan's laurels at the state fair, weighed in on the behalf of M. W. Savage in a series of comments to The *Journal.* "Instead of imposing on Savage in this way, " he wrote, "I should say the authorities ought to lend every encouragement to a man who has done so much for state horse interests, and that has also benefited the whole community by taking the old exposition building off our hands and making it the public attraction and convenience that it's bound to be."

The typical horse in Minnesota was valued at about $40, according to MacLean. "Mr. Savage has acted like a gentleman and an honest citizen in this matter. He turned in a valuation of $261 each, I believe, on all his horses, including Dan Patch. That's some six times as much as any other man is giving as the taxable value of a horse in Minnesota."

The board was not much convinced by MacLean's argument, nor by the pleas of other horse-owners who defended Savage's cause. After further hemming and hawing, it placed a total value on the International

Stock Farm stable at $22,500. Dan alone was figured to be worth $10,000 for tax purposes. The board assessed the other forty-seven horses, including Online, Directum, and Roy Wilkes, at $12,500.

The assessment would remain upon Dan's head for years to come, though it never sat well with Savage. He would later point out that "in Indiana and other states, the best harness horses are taxed at $1,500 at the most. ... No other harness horse in the United States was ever taxed at $10,000."

Of course, there was no other harness horse quite like Dan Patch.

## October Surprise

Dan Patch opened the month of October in an unremarkable way. On a wet track in Cincinnati, before a large crowd, he turned in a time of 2:01 ¾. It was a solid effort, but it broke no records and reflected the gray afternoon.

At Lexington two weeks later, however, Dan smashed the world's record for a four-wheeled wagon before four thousand screaming fans. On a fast track, with two runners spurring him on, Dan clipped a full two and a half seconds off the record pace, dropping it from 2:01 ½ to 1:59 ¼. It was a remarkable display of his prowess, pulling a four-wheeled vehicle at a clip that only two other horses had achieved pulling a much lighter sulky. And it was pointedly observed by the wire service report from Lexington that "no wind shields or any other speed accelerators [were] used for Dan Patch in his record-breaking trial."

From Lexington, Dan was shipped to Memphis, Tennessee, for a week of exhibitions at one of the finest racing facilities in the country. It had been built by G. K. C. Billings, a local streetcar mogul who also, perhaps not coincidentally, had recently purchased a filly named Lou Dillon who was widely considered the premier trotter in the country.

In 1903 Dillon had been the first trotter to crack the two-minute barrier. Her only real competitor at the time was Major Delmar, who had also broken the two-minute barrier later that summer, albeit with the aide of a large wind-screen in the fashion of Prince Direct. A few weeks before Dan Patch's arrival in Memphis, the two trotters had squared off in a major showdown. But deprived of his wind-screen, Major Delmar was no match for Lou Dillon. The filly chewed up her opponent that afternoon and took home the gold Memphis Cup as the year's top trotter.

At that point the focus of attention shifted to Dan Patch. On October 22, he took to the track with 8-to-5 odds against him breaking the world's pacing record. Yet Savage himself was convinced that his horse had a record time in him that day. The reasoning was simple. "Dan Patch had not been urged to do his very best by Mr. McHenry in his trials against time this summer, and I knew that once he was called upon to do 1:57 he would make good. When it was definitely settled that Dan would start at Memphis, I told Mr. McHenry to go the limit."[4]

And McHenry did. With three runners accompanying him—one ahead driven by a man named Scott Hudson, and two behind steered by drivers named Mack and Banta—Dan took off. A ballad would soon appear in newspapers across the country describing what happened next. It was called "Dan Patch's Reply"—a direct answer to the challenge of Prince Direct:

> *Scott paced me, Mack chased me, Banta clattered behind*
> *At a clip that was flying for one of my kind;*
> *All the quarters were 'flat twenty-nine' except one,*
> *And the mile fifty-six and a quarter when done.*

1:56 ¼! Almost three full seconds faster than Dan had ever raced before, and three-quarters of a second faster than Prince Direct's shield-aided, hopped-up, hopple-guided record from the month before. The crowd in Memphis was direct in its approval. "Seldom has a horse received the ovation which greeted Dan Patch as Driver McHenry pulled up in front of the grandstand and doffed his cap. The grandstand indulged in a roar which could have been heard across the Mississippi and kept it up until the horse had left the track."

"The champion of 'auto-trotto-yachtic' pacing retired to his corner," wrote one horse scribe. "There were no more challenges. There was no need of a race." A front page cartoon in the *Minneapolis Journal* drove the point home. It pictured Dan Patch, admiring himself in a mirror, with a crown on his head labeled, "World's Pacing Record." The caption beneath read, "Is My Crown on Straight? Well, I rather guess yes, and it doesn't need any wind shield to keep it there."

Just five days later, on October 27, Dan was on the track again in Memphis. This time, his intention was to top his own, and the world's, best marks for pacing the half-mile and pacing the mile to wagon. In races scheduled only forty-five minutes apart, he eclipsed both standards in a spectacular display of speed and grit. First came the half, which Dan clocked in fifty-six seconds. Less than an hour later, he was back at it, lugging McHenry around the track in a wagon to the time of 1:57 ¼, a full two seconds better than his record-breaking time eleven days earlier in Lexington.

Once again, the crowd in Memphis was ecstatic. The grandstand demonstration for his half-mile record was no less enthusiastic than the one he'd received for his mile a few days earlier, but even this was eclipsed by the uproar that followed his wagon record. The horse racing fans of Memphis had seen three world records from Dan Patch in a week's time. In fact, he seemed hardly the worse for wear after having smashed two records in a single afternoon.

Dan had two more exhibitions that fall—in Birmingham, Alabama, the week of November 6, and in Macon, Georgia, in the last week of November. In Birmingham he ran a 2:03 ¼, breaking the world's record for the mile paced on a half-mile track, and in Macon, he broke the mile record for pacers pulling an old-fashioned high-wheeled sulky with a time of 2:04 ¾. On that same afternoon Dan also set a new record for pacers in the two-mile run, finishing in 4 minutes, 17 seconds.

It was hard to imagine a more spectacular two months of racing. From mid-October to the end of November, Dan Patch had set seven world record times in eight exhibitions against time. It was no exaggeration to say that the horseracing world stood in awe.

"There has never been another like him," wrote one fan to Savage. "As he appeared at Memphis he was, literally, a grander sight than ever before, not simply because he paced in 1:56 ¼, but because he was in such superb physical condition, such a magnificent specimen of his kind, that no horseman could see him and leave his admiration unspoken."[5]

## Return to Nicollet Avenue

Eleven months after his first triumphant arrival in Minnesota, Dan Patch made his second parade from the train station down Nicollet Avenue to the Savage house on Park Avenue. Home from his astounding season on the circuit, Dan was once again met at the depot by a crowd of about two thousand, along with the same greeting committee that had hosted his arrival the previous January—The Journal's Newsboy Band, the mounted police, R. F. Jones, and the drivers of the Minneapolis Driving Club in their fancy carriages. A float proclaiming Dan "the real and only champion pacer" preceded him up the street, and Marion Willis Savage was in a carriage behind.

There was one notable absence, however, a single shadow clouding the magnificent end of the 1903 season. Myron McHenry had parted company with M. W. Savage. The year-long experiment of two strong-willed men trying to jointly govern the career of a single champion horse had ended in failure.

The reasons for the break-up were evident to all those who had observed their association during the racing season. The Savage camp accused McHenry, a married man, of womanizing, hanging too closely to a disreputable circle of track friends, and boozing. In the eyes of the Methodist who was doing the counting, that was a solid three strikes. The fact that McHenry, with his long experience in the horseracing world, tended to take a dim view of Savage's knowledge of horses and their training, only added to the friction.

Though his dedication to the cause of championship racing was undoubtedly sincere, McHenry won few points with Savage for condemning the manner in which Dan Patch was being "circused" to promote International Stock Food products, and he refused to play any part in such activities. Nor did his criticisms of Dan's heavy stud season and exhibition schedule wear well with the horse's owner. In the words of harness racing writer, John Hervey, "nature never intended two men like Mr. Savage and McHenry to get along together."

So McHenry was suddenly gone, and with him went the final link to Dan Patch's salad days in Indiana and his days of racing heats on the Grand Circuit. He was now fully a creature of Marion Savage's International stable, and, as if to confirm that fact, Savage chose as Dan's new trainer, the man who had overseen his care at the Savage farm, Harry Hersey.

The choice left many in the world of horseracing shaking their heads. McHenry had been the sport's premier driver, a man whose name was known by every horseman in the country. More than a few enthusiasts felt that Dan Patch's success was due as much to the talents of his driver as it was to the innate ability of the horse.

In contrast, Harry Hersey was a nobody, a Minnesota hick who'd never raced on a Grand Circuit track in his life. And this was the man M. W. Savage had chosen to race Dan Patch in the 1904 season?

If Marion Savage was worried about the future of his prize horse, he didn't show it. When a *Journal* reporter inquired if Dan was going to winter at the farm or in the city, Savage sounded downright cocky as he replied, "I guess Dan is still good enough for a buggy horse, and I will use him at the house this winter."

An electric automobile on Hennepin Avenue

# 10

# Doomed to Early Death

In August 1902, a farmer working along the Minnetonka Road west of Minneapolis had his horses startled by a passing automobile. His response was extreme. In a fit of what later would come to be known as "road-rage," the plowman pulled a small-caliber rifle from beneath his buckboard and shot the car driver in the back as the auto tried to speed away.

According to the *Minneapolis Journal*, the victim, a prominent citizen of the city, was painfully but not seriously injured and had decided not to press charges in order "to escape the chaffing he knew he would receive if the incident ever became known."[1]

The *Journal* was less disposed to let the shooter off so lightly. "It is said that a number of farmers living along the road have agreed to do everything in their power to discourage automobilists, but such drastic measures as shooting a man in the back will scarcely be indorsed by many of them," said the paper. "Such an offense, if the offender should be brought to court, would result in a heavy penitentiary sentence, and despite the action of the first victim, it is by no means a joking matter."

The dawn of the Automobile Age was a sometimes volatile moment in history, and incidents of violence between car owners and bystanders were not confined to rural America. A year and a half later, the *Journal* reported that in New York City "there have been numerous assaults upon automobile parties by boys and young men living in the unsavory parts of town. Several women and children have been fatally injured by flying sticks and stones. Machines have been wrecked by the score until finally they are no longer driven through sections of the city."

In Philadelphia and Boston similar incidents had occurred. In The *Journal's* estimation the problem was that "in the minds of the ignorant, the embittered poor and ... the youthful criminal classes ... the automobile is an offensive embodiment of the cruelty and the selfishness of wealth." The blame, according to the paper, was not all with the benighted poor. "Reckless driving, with its attendant injuries to innocent persons ... stirs up class hatred and bitterness." The remedy for these problems "lies with the automobilists themselves. A little more thought for others, a little more willingness to divide the 'right of road' with slower vehicles and pedestrians and a little less of the mad desire to violate all the laws regulating speed will solve the problem."[2]

Back in Minnesota one veteran of the Civil War was so enraged by the antics of motorists that he all but declared that a state of war existed between "automaniacs" and the rest of the users of the state's roads: "An irrepressible conflict between people who maintain and of necessity use the highways, and the few who confiscate them for pleasure, is in progress. Every day in the year this murderous minority run over one or more victims, always maiming and often killing, until the casualties equal those of war. Every time one is obliged to risk an assault from these death-dealing monsters, the same sentiments stir the breast that control in battle—terror, anger, or grim determination, according to temperament. In stating this fact I am not drawing on imagination for I wear an iron button and was in Banks' Red River expedition over forty years ago, where fighting and death from exposure was as constant as the automobile holocaust."[3]

Holocaust or not, automobiles continued to make inroads into American society. Even as Dan Patch began his rise to glory in the first years of the new century, the inexorable shift to a horseless age had begun. Automobile production and usage rose steeply during the first decade of the twentieth century. In 1898 there were approximately eight hundred licensed chauffeurs in New York State; ten years later, that figure was estimated at twenty-five thousand. In that same span, the amount of capital invested in the automobile industry in New York had jumped from $6.5 million to $450 million.[4]

The arrival of the horseless carriage made an immediate impact on a number of occupations. Automobiles were being used in Minnesota by the U.S. Post Office to carry mail as early as 1901, while the police in Minneapolis used an automobile to search for a suspect for the first time in 1906. Engined firetrucks were being advocated for use in the Twin Cities as early as 1902, "stove-wagons" or "auto-trucks" were being exhibited at a Minneapolis auto show in 1907, the mayor of Minneapolis suggested using automobiles as ambulances in 1906. In Albert Lea, Minnesota, an automobile replaced the town streetcar in 1900.

Autos were attractive to the sporting world as well. They had made a tentative appearance at the Minnesota State Fair in 1900 with a series of races on the harness track. However, they didn't make a great impression with the fair management. "'We did put on a few auto races two years ago,'" said an unnamed source in the *Journal* in August 1902, "'and what was the result? Why the chauffeurs got out on the track and we simply couldn't get them off. They wouldn't listen to our protests, persisted in careering around the track, keeping off the horses, and the result was that the day's program of harness races was spoiled.'" [5]

As the transportation needs of the country continued to grow during the first years of the century, automobile use burgeoned—but the use of horses grew as well. In fact, the number of horses owned and employed in the United States rose steadily during the first decade of the twentieth century. In 1902 there were about 16.5 million horses in the country, valued at just under one billion dollars. Five years later those numbers had climbed to almost 20 million horses, valued at 1.8 billion dollars. The increased valuation of individual horses from about $58 per animal in 1902 to $94 per horse in 1907 suggests that horses and the horse trade remained a thriving industry.

Barrett and Zimmerman horse lot, ca 1900

The Twin Cities had a particularly solid horse trading market—the largest in the Northwest. Centered in the Midway area between Saint Paul and Minneapolis, the business was led by the biggest horse-selling firm in the region, Barrett & Zimmerman, which made enormous profits at the turn of the century by selling horses to the U.S. Army during the Spanish-American War, to the British government during the Boer War, and to the Japanese during its war with Russia. It had a 200,000-square-foot barn and an adjoining feed lot of forty acres. In 1901 it handled the sale of 15,000 horses, an average of more than forty a day.[6]

While the advance of the automobile was difficult to ignore during the early years of the century, few observers were quite willing to write obituaries for the age of horse travel. An editor at The *Minneapolis*

*Journal* suggested the prevailing sensibility when he wrote: "There will be horses raised and horses used for many a generation to come, despite the perfection of the auto-truck ... and the increasing number of autos proper that are displacing the horse of speed." The impact of the auto was being overestimated in his view. "The telephone companies have cut into the telegraph business and have undoubtedly checked a growth in the extension of telegraph lines, but the telegraph companies are still doing business ... The automobile has, indeed, affected the horse business materially, but the horse is far from being a dead one."[7]

## "Toast to the King"

The popularity of Dan Patch was evidence of that. As he prepared for the 1904 season in the wake of his record-breaking exhibitions the year before, Dan remained very much in the public eye and more popular than ever. R. F. "Fish" Jones's *Northwestern Horseman and Stockman* published an essay calling attention to the great strides that Minnesota had taken as a home to blooded stock horses, and beside it was a poem called "Toast to a King" which read in part:

> *Up with it, down with it----*
> *Here's to Dan Patch*
> *The king of all horses; nowhere is his match*
> *Unbeaten by rivals, undaunted by time*
> *No horse shall e'er equal this prince in his prime.*

Dan would now be traveling like a prince, too. Over the winter, M. W. Savage had furnished a private railway car for his prize steed's journeys. It was painted a brilliant white, with nearly life-sized portraits of Dan on both sides of the car along with suitably bold advertisements for the International Stock Food Company. The pacer was given half the space as his private apartment, while the other half of the car was occupied by the horses, who would serve as "runners" in his exhibitions. Rubber pads on the floor of the car cushioned Dan's cross-country journeys, and he typically traveled with as many as four grooms to attend to his needs.

Dan Patch standing beside his private railroad car, with the Taj in the background

His winter home at the International Stock Food Farm was likewise taking on the appearance of a princely abode. His stall at the central barn on the property was decked out like a Victorian parlor with lace curtains on stall windows and a picture of his sire, Joe Patchen, hanging on the wall. Dan's ribbons and trophies were carefully arranged around him, and at least one groom slept just outside the stable door while a night watchman patrolled the grounds.

Before going into training for the 1904 exhibition season, Dan received fifty-seven mares at the farm in Savage, a breeding schedule that would no doubt have made Myron McHenry shudder. At $300 a session, however, it was easy to understand why M. W. Savage felt little constraint in the matter. The sum of $17,000 for one spring's worth of work went a long way to recouping his initial investment on the champion. And the 1904 race season hadn't even begun.

Because the schedule for the previous year had emphasized the Grand Circuit and the East Coast tour of harness racing venues,

Savage now decided to give the southern and western regions of the country a glimpse at Dan Patch. He would begin his exhibition season in Indianapolis, near Dan's old stomping grounds at Oxford, and then head to Des Moines, Lincoln, Milwaukee, Kansas City, Chicago, Grand Rapids, Michigan, Memphis, and Winnipeg.

There was considerable conjecture among the racing cognoscenti about the merits of Dan's new driver, Harry Hersey. (There were doubts, too, about how to spell his last name: most accounts give it as Hershey and some as Herschel). But the *Minneapolis Journal* was willing to give him the benefit of the doubt. "He is a little man, cool and determined, and probably knows more of Dan's whims and moods than any other living man," wrote the paper. Savage was so confident in the new man driving his horse that he predicted Hersey would take Dan as low as 1:52 in 1904.

Yet questions remained. Hersey had begun his career as a twenty-five year old groomsman

Henry Hersey

for a farm in upstate New York. Nine years later, in 1901, he was working for Savage, an unknown trainer in a midwestern state that was not well-known as a racetrack hotbed or a breeding ground for harness horses. Now this obscure driver was about to take the reins of the finest harness horse in the country. It was fair to ask what sort of experience qualified Harry Hersey for the role.

## A Contretemps

Noticeably absent from Dan Patch's schedule for the fall was a stop at the Minnesota State Fair. Exactly what happened to sour relationships between M. W. Savage and the Fair Board is unknown, but sour they were.

According to Will Savage, the reason that Dan Patch was not appearing at the fair was that he hadn't been asked until it was too late. "The facts are these," he told the *Horseman and Stockman*, in August 1904. "Dan Patch gave a speed exhibition at the state fair last year and everyone knows what a large crowd he drew on the first day, always considered the poorest day of the fair. The fair people had all of last fall, all of last winter and spring to make a request for Dan to appear at their 1904 fair but they did not make any such request. On the contrary, it was commonly reported on the streets that certain members of the state fair board had stated that Dan was a local horse and that they did not want him."

In July, said Savage, he had received a phone call from the fair secretary stating that they would like to have Dan appear on Saturday, the last day of this year's fair.

The problem was that Dan was already booked for that day, a fact everyone in the local horse business knew. "Some two months before this it had been published in our city papers that Dan had been engaged for the Nebraska State Fair, which occurs the same week as the Minnesota State Fair," wrote Savage, who then implied that the Fair Board was simply covering its tracks for the benefit of the public, which it knew would be interested in his horse appearing at the fair. "In this way they would be in a very smooth position, as they could tell people they had asked for Dan and could not get him."

Trying to come up with a workable compromise that would allow Minnesota harness fans an opportunity to see Dan Patch that summer, "Fish" Jones scheduled two days of racing at the Hamline fair grounds for mid-August, two weeks before the state fair. The first day would be given over to an exhibition of auto racing and the second to the harness horses, including Dan Patch.

A week before the scheduled event, however, the Fair Board nixed the idea. If Dan Patch was not going to appear at the 1904 State Fair, there was no way it would let him appear in an exhibition on the fairgrounds two weeks before the event. Whether or not the fair board was playing power games with Savage and Jones, making sure that it controlled the date and manner in which Dan appeared at the fair, is difficult to judge. It may simply have felt a little stung by its own bad judgment the year before, when it allowed Savage to make a killing by taking a percentage of the profits on the first day of the fair rather than a straight exhibition fee as he had originally requested. For whatever reason, the board made little effort to get Dan Patch on the fairgrounds a year after he'd wowed the locals in his first Minnesota race. Jones's harness racing exhibition was off, and to a reporter for the *Minneapolis Journal*, Jones angrily declared that "he had done all human power can do to bring about [the race], and he trusts [the public] may fully appreciate and lay the blame entirely where it belongs."

State Fair auto racing ca. 1905

The state fair board granted use of the track to just the automobiles for the two days scheduled in mid-August, and 10,000 fans turned out to watch racers like A. C. Webb and Lem Knissley reach speeds almost twice as fast as the ones Dan Patch posted on the track. The autos traveled at more than a mile a minute as they sped around the Hamline track in one-, two-, and three-mile "dashes," driving sixty-horsepower vehicles, including Ramblers, Packards, and Pope Toledos.

Meanwhile, Dan Patch had returned from his opening date at Indianapolis, where he'd paced 2:02 ¼ on a rain-soaked track, to the farm in Savage. Instead of Hamline, he would now head to Des Moines for an exhibition and then on to Lincoln for his stop at the Nebraska State Fair. There would be no Dan Patch speed exhibition in Minnesota in 1904.

To add to these late summer concerns, the worst storm in the Twin Cities' history passed through Minneapolis and St. Paul on the evening of August 22, and Savage's town home was struck by lightning. It caught fire, doing considerable damage to its upper floors.

The house was saved, and Savage was far from the worst victim of the storm. Sweeping through the towns west of Minneapolis and going right through the heart of city's business district, the tornadic winds shattered 145 of the 162 double-plated window panes in Donaldson's famed Glass Block Department Store, doing an estimated $100,000 worth of damage. St. Paul was equally hard hit, with severe damage to its famed High Bridge on the Mississippi River. In all, more than a dozen area residents were killed by the storm and scores were injured.

## Crisis in Topeka

Meanwhile, Dan Patch was off to Des Moines, where he set the state record for the mile on a half-mile track. His time, however, 2:06, was far from his best.

In Nebraska, twenty thousand fairgoers watched the stallion race on another half-mile track. Again he set a state record, and again, at 2:05 ¼, he'd done better elsewhere.

It was still early in the season, and the tracks he was working on were not of the quality found on the Grand Circuit. All the same, he'd had such a spectacular season in 1903, particularly at the end, that it was hard not to anticipate a record every time he set foot on the racetrack.

At the Wisconsin State Fair in Milwaukee a huge throng of fifty thousand squeezed into the grandstands as well as the inside and outside of the track to watch Dan Patch beat the clock. He did 2:03 on a rainy turf, and few left the grounds disappointed in his performance. On the other hand, following what was seen as yet another slightly sub-par performance, racing enthusiasts renewed their speculations about the connection between Dan's slower times and the skills of the newcomer driving him, Harry Hersey. Was it just a coincidence that Dan's times were off, or, in the words of John Hervey, was this an indication "that Dan Patch's future lay in his past"? [8]

Dan was scheduled to do a time trial on September 14 at the Kansas State Fair, and he was shipped to Topeka. In his first night on the fairgrounds, his handlers found him in obvious distress in his stable. He was feverish and sweaty, and upon inspection his abdomen was discovered to be swollen. Hersey was there, heading a contingent of handlers including Dan's groomsman, Charlie Plummer. Savage, who was back in Minnesota, was immediately notified and given a preliminary diagnosis, which was also sent out via telegraph across the country. It wasn't good. The King of the Pacers had a strangulated hernia according to the report. The problem was so serious that there was little that could be done for the horse except to comfort him.

A strangulated hernia is a particularly dangerous rupture of the intestinal lining. Somehow a portion of Dan's bowel had become trapped in the abdominal wall, cutting off the flow of blood to the protrusion. In most such cases, gangrene was quick to follow upon the loss of blood to the strangulated area. The condition was not only extremely painful, but without surgery or miraculous intervention, it was almost always fatal.

In 1904 veterinary medicine was in its infancy. Veterinary schools were few and far between, and the myriad "horse doctors" and "empirics" who tended to livestock in small towns throughout the country were almost invariably self-taught. In the years between 1872 and 1900, as few as ninety-seven veterinarians with genuine degrees practiced in the state of Minnesota, and few of these had experience in surgery. In fact, surgery on strangulated hernias, even in humans, was a rare and difficult procedure in the day, and one fraught with the prospect of sepsis. The fact of the matter was that although Dan Patch was a valuable and much-loved horse, no one was going to perform surgery on him.

Hersey, who had not slept a wink since Dan's first signs of discomfort, sadly wired a reporter for the *Minneapolis Journal* that "Dan has no chance on earth." On September 13 in the Twin Cities and elsewhere across the country, the story was headline news: "Dan Patch Fights Gamely With Death," "King of Pacers is Doomed to Early Death," "Dan Patch Sick," "Dan Patch Dying in Topeka, Kansas."

From his summer home in Bloomington, M. W. Savage wired for the best veterinarians in the region to attend his horse in Topeka, and then headed to Kansas himself. The doctors arrived from Omaha, Chicago, and Kansas City, joining a growing group of newspapermen, trainers, and drivers from other stables who stood outside Dan's stable on a deathwatch, swapping stories of his prowess on the track. The crowd would grow suddenly quiet, however, whenever the door of the box stall opened and someone emerged with a report of Dan's condition.

Inside the stall, said the *St. Paul Globe*, Dan was "propped up on a bed as soft as any in the land, with shaded lanterns casting their shadows over [the horse]." The bathos, according to this report, was thick: "Always strangely intelligent, Dan Patch in his sickness is almost human, and when he raises his broad, bony head and surveys the group around him the rough and ready stable boys sob and weep."

Dan appeared to rally toward evening, "but as darkness fell the horsemen skilled in the ills and ways of the horse shook their heads as it was evident that Dan was suffering acutely. Occasionally the big black groaned, and the anxious crowd of watchers outside the stall gazed at one another as if some human being was in his last agonies instead of a horse."

Then came some good news. Dr. Robert Moore of the Kansas City Veterinary College, one of the top-notch vets contacted by Savage, had examined Dan late in the morning of September 13, and he declared that the horse was not suffering from a strangulated hernia. Rather, it was impacted bowels, which had probably been caused by eating oat chaff.

The bad news was that the mahogany stallion was still extremely sick and the prognosis was as desperate as it had been before. "The conditions gradually grew worse during the afternoon until about 4 p.m. the pulse rate reached more than 100 and his temperature was 105°," Dr. Moore later reported. "The heart grew so feeble that the pulse could not be taken at the jaw and the rate could only be determined by listening to the heart beats. A cold perspiration covered the entire body much of the time and the pain was almost continuous ... At this time owing to the inflammatory condition and the extreme weak heart, the prognosis was very unfavorable. From 4 to 6 p.m. I had little or no hope of his recovery."[9]

Savage arrived at the stable later that day. Exactly what happened at this point has been colored by legend. It is said that Savage, brushing aside suggestions that Dan Patch was on his deathbed, immediately drew a vial of his own International Colic Cure ('The only Colic Cure sold with a Cash Guarantee') from his pocket and called in some handlers and vets to help persuade Dan to take it. Then he asked to be left alone with the horse. Savage proceeded to bed down with Dan in the stable, petting, comforting, and praying over the horse throughout the night.

The following morning one of the handlers tiptoed into the stall, and a few seconds later came back out, beaming, "Anyone know where we can get some apples?" he asked.[10]

Whatever the actual course of events may have been, Dan Patch was suddenly making a remarkable recovery. Early the next morning, Hersey telegraphed the *Minneapolis Journal* that Dan was "very sick, but case is not hopeless." The horse continued to improve, and the deathwatch came to an abrupt end. The best vets in the West were soon on their way home, and in a matter of just four days, Dan Patch was well enough to be shipped back to his stall in Savage for recuperation at the International Stock Food Farm.

That it was not M. W. Savage and his International Colic Cure that saved Dan can perhaps be judged by the fact that Savage himself never reported that it did. And he was not a man to be shy about trumpeting the healthy and felicitous affects of his products. In *Dan Patch 1:55*, published the year after Dan's brush with death, Savage offers the testimonial of Dr. Moore, describing Dan's dire conditions on the morning of the thirteenth. To the rhetorical question, "What Restored Dan Patch in Six Weeks?" printed beneath Moore's report, Savage trumpets his International Stock Food, not his colic cure. Dan was given the feed supplement four times a day at a dosage three times the norm, according to the ad copy. In just three weeks from the first day of his illness, Dan Patch would once again be ready to race.

# 11

# National Pet

an Patch's reputation as a race-horse had been stellar almost from his first competitive turn around the track, but after his illness in Topeka, there was a subtle shift in the public perception of him. Dan had previously seemed merely invincible—a great athlete performing in his prime. After nearly losing him to a prosaic illness, racing fans now began to view the horse as a vulnerable creature, and this made his talents all the more special and deepened public affection for him. It was as if people suddenly understood that one day the headlines announcing Dan's imminent death might not be followed by stories of his miraculous recovery. If Dan Patch was an athlete they would want to tell their grandchildren they had seen, they had better get out to the track and see him.

At the same time, racing experts grew a little more cautious about trumpeting Dan's achievements. No one seemed to doubt his talents, but the way he was being handled and exhibited by Savage was beginning to draw more widespread criticism. It was felt that he had entered "show business" and was now surrounding himself on the track with a squadron of pacing horses, including a lead runner carrying a "dirt shield" attached to his sulky which looked an awful lot like a smaller version of  Prince Direct's controversial windbreak.[1]

And as to the question of how good Dan Patch actually was, the answer from the racing crowd grew more equivocal. "The horse is a wonder," said one expert in the *Chicago Daily News*, "and Dan Patch, in my opinion, will stand alone for several years as the fastest pacer in the world." And yet: "Without a doubt the windshield helps by several seconds."

Meanwhile, Alfred Reeves, Secretary of the New York Driving Club told the *New York Times*, "Prince Alert has gone with wind shield, and there is no reason why every other horse in the country should not be permitted to do likewise … Nevertheless, I do believe that the governing body of the sport should make a rule stating just how many square inches of the wind shield should be carried by the pacemaker in front, so that wind shields should come within a reasonable limit. Records so made should, in my opinion, be placed in a class by themselves, but by no means should be discredited."[2]

In the winter of 1904 the National Trotting Association decided to follow this policy and limit the size of the shields carried on the sulkies of the pace-setters. They also decided to place a prominent asterisk beside all the records set on the harness tracks the year before, including each and every one of Dan Patch's record-breaking races.

Will Savage claimed that the decision made no difference to him. "I am quite satisfied," he said to the *Minneapolis Journal*, "since the [National Trotting Association] committee has allowed the records made by Dan Patch. I do not care about the requirement that these marks shall be recorded with a distinguishing symbol."

Savage's sensitivity to the asterisks would grow with the passing years, however, as it would toward the niggling reporters who seemed never to tire of describing the lead runners and dirt shields involved in Dan Patch's performances.

## Back in the Harness

Dan's first go after his illness was at the Illinois State Fair in Springfield. Despite pacing on the eve of "Chicago Day" at the 1904 World's Fair in St. Louis, Dan still drew Illini fans into the Springfield track by the carloads. Fifty thousand people came out to see him race, and they could not have cared less about shields and pace-setters, except in so far as they added to the excitement of Dan's race against time.

"Depots at night were packed with people waiting for their trains. Specials were run on all roads and there were the old time scenes of thousands of people waiting patiently after a day's tramping," according to the *Springfield News*. His appearance saved the Illinois State Fair finances for that year: "The immense crowds in the city yesterday were big enough to make the fair a success, and there will be enough money to pay all the expenses … If Daniel knew and appreciated how much the state fair is indebted to him, he might experience an enlargement of the head."

Yet Dan set no racing records in Springfield. In fact, at 2:04, his time was far from his best, though it seemed to matter little to those attending. "Those who saw Dan Patch go were repaid for their time and efforts," reported the Springfield paper. Despite the fact that "the horse did not break any records … he is still a national pet. He can still command the plaudits and worship of the millions and from their pocketbooks he can extract the dollars for a chance to see him."

Though expectations for the 1904 season were diminished because of Dan's recent illness, he would nevertheless continue to draw crowds. He would also prove remarkably resilient. In Memphis at the end of October, Dan showed that he was not only fully recovered from his bout with indigestion, but that no season of his would pass without a run at the record book.

The meet in Tennessee was a two-week-long series of races that marked the end of the Grand Circuit season, and it had already provided a great deal of high drama before Dan Patch entered the scene. On October 18 the two leading trotters in the country, Lou Dillon and Major Delmar, were scheduled for a rematch race for the Memphis Gold Cup, which Dillon had won the year before. Dillon was the filly owned by C. K. G. Billings, the millionaire owner of Memphis's streetcar system and builder of the very track that the horses were going to race on. She had been the first trotter to break the two-minute barrier, though Major Delmar had lost little time lowering the mark further with the help of a much larger windshield.

Delmar had been bred and trained in California. He was later purchased for $40,000 by Elmer Smathers, a New York sportsman, just before the two horses went head-to-head in the first Gold Cup. Easily cast as the out-of-town "villain" in the Memphis setting, Major Delmar had been having another fine 1904 season, and the race between the two trotters promised to be even more competitive than the previous year.

The race for the Cup was a best-of-three-heats match. In their first go, Major Delmar swamped Lou Dillon, trotting the mile in 2:05 to Dillon's 2:18 ½. The audience was shocked by the size of Delmar's victory and almost immediately began whispering about the condition of Lou Dillon at the end of the race. Something was wrong with the filly. She was said to have finished the first run trembling and in great distress, but she eventually pulled herself together and went out for a second heat.

Head-to-head through the first quarter of a mile in heat number two, the horses trotted together at a :30 ½ seconds clip, with Major Delmar taking a slight lead at the half. Suddenly the Memphis crowd was once again shocked, this time to see Lou Dillon slow and come to a complete stop. It was hard to believe, but a little more than a minute into the much-anticipated race, it was over—Major Delmar was taking home the Memphis Gold Cup as the best trotter of the year.

The head-shaking about Lou Dillon's performance and her race-day condition—or lack thereof—continued through that day and the rest of the meet. There was no explaining her performance. The day before the race, she had trotted a mile in 2:03; the day after the race, according to witnesses, she was fit-as-a-fiddle. What could have made her trot so poorly on the day of the races?

An answer—or at least an accusation—would come out months later. In the summer of 1905 the trainer of Major Delmar, recently dismissed by Elmer Smathers, confessed to giving Lou Dillon a bottle of champagne just before the race at the behest of Mr. Smathers. Just how he managed to do this and what effect it had on the races were questions that weren't immediately answered, but the charges were serious enough for a Grand Jury in Memphis to hand down an indictment against Major Delmar's owner.

To confuse matters even more, by that time Elmer Smathers no longer owned Major Delmar. He had been purchased soon after the Memphis race by none other than C. K. G. Billings, Lou Dillon's owner, at the annual Old Glory Auction in New York's Madison Square Garden.

Perhaps not surprisingly, Billings was no longer interested in pursuing the matter of the doping charge, but authorities in Memphis were. By the time the issue was fully adjudicated three years later, Smathers was acquitted and exonerated, but the world of harness racing was more than a little embarrassed by the whole sordid mess.

## Dan's Memphis Race

It was within this backdrop of doping whispers and gossip that Dan Patch paced that year in Memphis.

In fact it was the last race of the Memphis meet—October 26, 1904—and oddsmakers were giving even money that Dan couldn't break a two-minute mile. Aside from the fact that he hadn't done so all season, the horse was still only six-weeks removed from his death-watch in Topeka, and the still-unproven Harry Hersey would be at the reins as usual.

Hersey was given an additional burden by the American Trotting Association. In an attempt to standardize the weights of drivers in Grand Circuit events, it had fixed 150 pounds as the required weight for drivers in competition. Because he weighed just 131 pounds, Hersey was asked to tote an additional 19 pounds of lead weights sewn into the lining of his driving jacket.

Scott Hudson, the familiar driver of the lead pacer, sped to the front on the Memphis track at the signal from the starting judge with Dan Patch behind and a second pace horse at the side. The track was still new, and one of the fastest in the country, but the day—a trifle chilly, with a slight wind blowing—was not particularly conducive to racing.

The first quarter-mile was logged at 29 seconds, and the next at :28 ½, making a :57 ½ half. It was the sort of pace that made fans sit up and take notice. At the half, another familiar member of the Dan Patch pacing team, "Doc" Tanner, joined the original trio of drivers, making a quartet of racers speeding toward the finish. According to The *Memphis Scimitar*, "Hersey hugged the rail still closer with his charge until it seemed as if he would scrape the very paint off the fence." Together, they pushed Dan to a 29 second third-quarter mile, which brought forth a succession of cheers from the crowd.

"Rounding into the stretch," the story in the *Scimitar* continued, "Hersey swung his charge a little wide of the rail to follow in the wake of his pacemaker, and everyone who watched the oncoming of the flying quartet as they thundered down the stretch arose en masse and cheered until the very echo answered back."

There was soon more to cheer about. A sign was hung out from the judge's stand indicating that Hersey's stallion had just run a 1:56 mile! M. W. Savage raced forward to congratulate his driver before a wildly cheering crowd. Meanwhile, the report concluded, "Dan Patch, seemingly as modest, well behaved and looking as fresh as possible under the circumstances, quietly walked back in front of the stand, [where] Driver Hersey and his charge were surrounded and the mighty little man of new record fame was almost carried off on the shoulders of his admiring friends."

The Pike at the St. Louis World's Fair, 1904

## "Meet Me in St. Louis"

With a new world's record added to his already impressive resume, Dan Patch arrived at the 1904 World's Fair in St. Louis just as that almost year-long extravaganza was wrapping up.

The Fair had opened in April to commemorate the one-hundredth anniversary of the Louisiana Purchase. It was already a year behind schedule when its gates were first opened, and by the time Dan Patch and his retinue arrived, the celebration was less than a month from closing.

The St. Louis Fair was larger even than the famed 1893 Columbian Exposition in Chicago. In fact, no World's Fair before or since has been quite so expansive. Fifteen hundred buildings sprawled over nearly thirteen hundred acres of fairgrounds. Almost twenty million people attended the gathering from all corners of the globe, and its cost, fifteen million dollars, was equal to the price paid for the enormous land purchase it was celebrating.

Ice cream cones, peanut butter, sliced bread, Dr. Pepper, and hot dogs were all first made popular by food vendors at the St. Louis Fair.

There were grand buildings dedicated to the arts and industry; Thomas Edison managed the Palace of Electricity, which included nightly illuminations of over half a million electric light bulbs and sweeping beams of changing hues. A movie theater on the grounds offered many visitors their first view of a motion picture.

Among scores of exhibitions from foreign lands, there was an entire Irish Village, a Tyrolean Alp exhibit, and an exhibit from the Philippine Islands, which highlighted an indigenous tribe called the Igorots. The Igorots drew huge crowds of people, in part because they were partially clothed and also because they were rumored to be feasting on dogs provided by local St. Louis officials. Though there was no proof of the charge, the local Humane Society expressed its outrage. Meanwhile, vendors of the German sausage in a bun, being sold as "hot dogs," reported huge sales of the novelty item.

Native Americans on exhibit at the fair

A mile-long Pike featured hundreds of attractions, including the one horse in the country whose fame rivaled Dan Patch's.

Beautiful Jim Key was a phenomenon at the Fair and beyond. Trained by a former slave and self-taught veterinarian, Dr. William Key, Jim was widely credited with being an educated horse, who knew how to read, write, tell time, and do calculations. He had first gone on the road with Dr. Key in 1897 as part of Key's medicine show and had quickly established a reputation as a remarkably gifted animal. For the next eight years Beautiful Jim Key both wowed the crowds and moved them. The kindness of Dr. Key in raising Jim was said to be at the root of his gifts, and a burgeoning animal-protection movement championed both the horse and his gentle trainer. In turn, Jim became a "spokesman" for the cause of Humane Societies across the country, and brutalized and overburdened workhorses, in particular, benefited from his life and example. His appearance at the World's Fair marked the culmination of a distinguished career, and it was said that he was biggest attraction on the Pike.

As if all of the exhibits and wonders—the palaces, the Pike, and a giant Ferris Wheel capable of carrying more than two thousand riders— were not enough, the 1904 St. Louis World's Fair was also the site of the first American-held Olympic Games. The contests were held right on the fairgrounds with the American team dominating, although the Russo-Japanese War limited the number of nations participating to just twelve.

Given all of this activity and the fact that he arrived at the fair so late in the day, it's perhaps not surprising that for one of the few times in his career, Dan Patch was not the brightest star in the firmament. Still, M. W. Savage managed to create a catchy headline for his horse.

Just before he was scheduled to appear, St. Louis racing officials had sent a telegram to Savage in Memphis requesting that Dan's trial run be shifted to Sunday from Monday. Ever the good churchman, Mr. Savage wired back: "Sorry, but Dan Patch joined the Methodist church two years ago." There would be no Sunday races for the champion pacer.

On November 3, Dan Patch arrived at the fair grounds in his palatial car. That same day, Savage's quip grabbed a local headline. Back in Minneapolis the Wesley United Methodist Church, the congregation to which Savage belonged, caught wind of the remark, and before long they had voted to give Dan Patch his own numbered envelopes, thereby making him perhaps the only horse ever to become a member of the Methodist Church.[3]

Meanwhile, back in St. Louis, Dan ran what was for him a pedestrian 2:01 ¼ on a track that was described by his handlers as far less than ideal.

## Oklahoma

Dan Patch's second to the last exhibition of the season would turn out to be one of the most remarkable performances of his career—all the more notable because it began with such unremarkable prospects.

The Oklahoma City track was a half-mile oval, and Dan was scheduled to race there on November 17, against his own world-best time for a mile on a half-mile track, a record he'd set the year before in Birmingham. The oval was not particularly fast—its footing was soft and dusty the day of the race—but the weather was fine, and a capacity crowd of five thousand was expectant.

Two pacemakers were employed in the exhibition. The lead was taken by a runner named Cobweb, driven by Charley Dean; the side horse was Trolley, steered by an Oklahoma City driver named Doc Lundberg. Hersey, of course, was behind Dan Patch, and it was he who gave the signal to the judge's stand when his horse was ready for a go at the record.

It was quickly apparent to the crowd that Dan Patch was burning up the racecourse. He navigated the first quarter in :30 ¼ seconds and entered the stretch on his first lap at a blistering clip. He passed the half-mile in 1:00 ½—the record pace was 1:01—and everyone watching felt that they were seeing a record-setting run.

Through three-quarters of the race, the pace continued at this breakneck speed. A time of 1:30 ½ was announced, and the crowd was feverish with excitement.

But on the far side of the track, just a few seconds after he'd passed that third quarter mark, Dan hit a soft patch. Just as the "huzzas" from the announcement of the last quarter time were dying down, another cry was heard in the stands, "'He has broken! He has broken!'"

Dan's gait had been wrecked by the silky dirt. Though he made a quick recovery, there were audible groans from the stands. That soft spot had wrecked a potentially record-breaking run.

What happened next was given a breathless description in the Dan Patch yearbook of 1905, reprinted from the *Daily Oklahoman*. "Like a whirlwind he [raced] toward the wire," wrote an anonymous reporter, "and for the moment there [was] a wonderful quiet over the great throng" as Dan Patch came down the stretch. "Then as this matchless racing animal passed under the wire in 2:03 flat, lowering the world's record by one-quarter of a second, a mighty shout went up and five thousand people, under the sublime excitement of the moment, [became] frantic with joy."

Not only had he recovered from a near fall, Dan had actually paced the last eighth of a mile in a stunning thirteen seconds.

"Women cried and men and children shouted themselves hoarse, and there [was] a wild rush to the track when the wonderful animal [was] brought back in front of the grand stand. Driver Hersey ... besieged with a mob of delirious enthusiasts pressing forward to extend their congratulations, and Dan Patch, the idol of the American turf, [became] the center of an admiring throng."

The next night, entertaining reporters at an Oklahoma City hotel, Hersey would call the race "the most wonderful mile ever paced by a horse." Of the near disaster, he would say, "I felt certain he would fall. We were going so fast that the dirt was giving way under his feet, leaving him little chance to hold up. I felt sure he would turn into the fence."

That Dan went on to break the record seemed to amaze Hersey as much as everyone else in Oklahoma City. "No other horse in turf history ever broke in a trial of this kind and lowered a world's record," he said. "His work today shows that the world has never produced his equal."

## Home is Where the Heart Is

Before heading for home Dan Patch made one final appearance in Dallas, where he paced 2:01 on a mile-track. By the time he reached Minneapolis near the end of November, he had traveled over ten thousand miles, been seen by hundreds of thousands of people, broken two more racing records in an abbreviated racing season, and almost died from an impacted bowel. He'd also picked up a new traveling companion in Oklahoma: a bull terrier named Oklahoma Bill, who would remain Dan's stable pal for many years to come.

It had been quite a season, and Dan Patch was once again greeted with a parade up Nicollet Avenue, complete with band and throngs of spectators. The champion stallion would be spending a few weeks at M .W. Savage's town home before heading out to the farm and on to another season of stud work.

Back in Oklahoma City following his record-breaking dash, Henry Hersey had told the reporters, "He does well in our cold climate. He gets big and strong, feels fine and is jogged every day. He is a young horse, being eight years old, and there is not a pimple on him. I see no reason why he should not beat his own, the world's record of 1:56 during 1905, and we believe that the public will see some truly sensational miles by the great Dan next season."[4]

Dan Patch (covered in a white blanket) proceeds down Nicollet Avenue in November 1905.

Dan Patch Day in Toronto, 1905

# 12

# "The Alexander of the Horse World"

In an article for the magazine *Trotter and Pacer* at the end of the
1905 season, Harry Hersey offered a rare detailed description of
Dan Patch's training schedule. According to Hersey, the horse's
work began in the spring when Dan was asked to go a mile in 2:50 to
3:00 every other day for two weeks. He was then given two miles twice a
week for three weeks, which was increased to three or four times a week
until he had beaten 2:25. Then he was asked to go from 2:25 to 2:20
four times a week. During this period he also served mares regularly on
days when he was not working out.

After his stud season closed on June 1, Hersey went on, "Dan
commenced to beat 2:20." He was worked eight miles per week at a
pace ranging from 2:30 to 2:15, running the last half of this workout at

a fast clip. He then continued the same training until Dan was able to go in 2:10 with safety. About the middle of August, Dan was starting to show a good deal of form. And from the middle of August until his first engagement at the Minnesota State Fair on the first week in September, Hersey revealed that he "worked Dan five times better than 2:10 and twice better than 2:05, once in 2:04 ¼, with the last half in :59 seconds."

"Fish" Jones was more than a little impressed by Dan Patch's ability to perform at the levels he did at the start of the season, with just two months of hard prep work and a full season at the stud. "Where are the old trainers of champions and what do they think of taking a stallion from the breeding paddocks and with sixty days preparation repeat the first attempt at fast time, well below two minutes?" he asked rhetorically in the September 1905 edition of the *Horseman and Stockman*. According to Jones, "the game going gelding" Johnston had spent from January to October in preparation for his record 2:06 ¼, back in the 1880s. And Dan Patch made him look like a Piker.

The brevity of Dan's training schedule may have been unusual, yet Harry Hersey and Will Savage were confident Dan was ready to go when the Minnesota State Fair opened on Monday, September 4, 1905.

Expectations for another record-breaking season had never been higher in the Dan Patch camp and in the world of harness racing in general, as would be proven by the sheer number of fans who descended on the race tracks of America over the next two months to see how fast this horse could pace a mile. Dan's record-breaking runs in Memphis and Oklahoma City in the wake of his illness in Topeka had simply whetted the appetites of his fans for more fast times.

"Considering the brilliancy of his achievements in the past it would not have been surprising to the majority of horsemen if he had reached the zenith of his fame a year or two ago," wrote a turf reporter for the *Horseman* in early September 1905. "But last season under most adverse conditions he reduced his record and there is no question but that he will repeat that act again this year if no accident befalls him before he reaches Memphis."

## Back at Hamline

The Minnesota State Fair Board was mindful of the mistake it had made the previous year in neglecting to ask Dan to come to the fair until it was too late, and had booked him well in advance of the 1905 event. His exhibition race at the fair would open both those festivities and his own racing season.

As for the board's ill-conceived proposal of 1903 that Will Savage take a percentage of the first day's receipts rather than a purse—well, the fair committee would have to lie in that particular bed once again. Savage had done so well on that day, he adopted the practice of taking a percentage as standard practice and would do so again 1905.

On opening day of 1903, the day of Dan's first appearance at the fair, 32,000 went through the turnstiles of the Minnesota State Fair. The following year, without Dan Patch, the fair drew just 16,400 on opening day. As the 1905 Fair neared, the guess was that there would be a sizable increase in attendance, but just how large that boost would be, no one knew.

Then the gates opened, and the tide rolled in.

"It was thought that the opening day record of two years ago might be topped [but] nobody had an idea that the attendance would break all prior records, not only for opening day, but for any day of the week," reported the *St. Paul Pioneer Press* the day after the opening. "By 10 o'clock the crowd began arriving in earnest, and at noon the turnstile count showed attendance of 26,000. After that the people arrived in squads, companies and regiments, seemingly with no letup."[1]

Almost every railroad line coming into the Twin Cities ran specials into the fair. In addition, the regularly scheduled trains added cars to help accommodate the throngs. The Omaha Line brought in large crowds from Spooner, Wisconsin, and Duluth, picking up other passengers at stops along the way. The Soo Line brought in scads of people living between Rhinelander, Wisconsin, and St. Paul. The trains were so crowded that visitors traveling from the Dakotas and northern Minnesota couldn't find sleeping accommodations on any of the cars,

and harness fans arrived in packed trains from Iowa and even as far away as Illinois.

As noted by the *Pioneer Press*, the opening day attendance for 1904 had already been bested two hours into the fair's first day, and Dan Patch wasn't scheduled to race until late in the afternoon.

"By two o'clock there was a continuous stream of people at every gate seeking admittance," reported the St. Paul paper, "and a half hour later the throngs could not be admitted fast enough to prevent congestion."

There was no mistaking the chief attraction that first day, either. Once inside the gates, the crowds streamed toward the track, where the largest audience ever gathered for a race, or any other event at the fair, was assembling.

A massive crowd at the Minnesota State Fair grandstand

"Not an available space which might hold a human being was unoccupied in the grandstand. The paddock was crowded with people who could not secure a better point of vantage and the infield was crowded up and down the stretch. The hill at the head of the enclosed track was packed with humanity and the 'rail birds' ranged way down the back stretch."

An initial head count for that first day of the fair was put at 75,000. The final figure was actually 63,799 paying visitors, according to the *Minneapolis Tribune*, a difference between first day tickets on 1905 and 1904 of nearly 50,000. The increase in the gate receipts, as reported by the *Pioneer Press*, amounted to a bump of almost $26,000.

In subsequent years a story emerged in several publications that the Fair Association had tried to convince Savage to take $5,000 instead of the full sum he was owed by contract, but Savage laughed at the idea. He also laughed at a subsequent offer of $7,500, and a final bid of $10,000 from the Fair Board. Why would he take anything less than he and Dan had earned?

The point of the story, that the Fair Board was not likely to get the best of M. W. Savage, carries the ring of truth. The dollar figure itself matches the actual difference in gate receipts between the 1904 and 1905 Minnesota fairs. Because this year represented the single biggest leap in first-day attendance between a pair of fairs and because we know Savage frequently signed contracts arranging exhibition fees based on Dan Patch's ability to boost attendance, it seems likely that the horse and Will Savage actually brought home something near $21,500 for one day's work at the 1905 Minnesota State Fair—$400,000 in modern currency. If so, this would be the single biggest payday in Dan Patch's racing career.

## They're Off!

It was around 2 p.m. when Dan appeared, took a few turns around the oval, and then returned to the stables until the moment his timed pacing was set to start. He was brought back out on the track at 4:30 accompanied by two runners, Cobweb and Trolley, driven by a pair of experienced horsemen.

The track was not in the best of shape—a week's worth of rain had dampened it prior to the fair and estimates were that it was three seconds slow. Considered opinion suggested that it would be impossible for Dan to beat his own track record from two years before, though few of the spectators hoped for anything less.

After returning to the track, Hersey, as usual resplendent in his white satin coat, made three false starts before nodding to the judge's stand that he and Dan Patch were ready to go. The audience, spilling over the grandstand, the hillsides, the paddocks and infield, roared its approval as Dan passed the start wire and took off in the company of his pacesetters on his first heat of the season.

The first quarter passed easily enough, though Dan was in such fine form that Hersey had to yell at the front runner to get in gear. This was Cobweb, one of the pacesetters from the season before. It was a thirty-second split, and Hersey wanted more speed from his leader. Unfortunately the backstretch was soft, and Dan followed his first quarter with an even slower second, doing :30 ½.

For the third quarter, Dan was moving so well that once again he rode up onto the sulky in front of him and Hersey wound up twice imploring Driver Hudson and Cobweb to move it along. The time for the quarter was a blistering :28 ¾ and could have been faster.

Likewise the final split. Again down the stretch, Hersey had to pull Dan out a little, at the risk of causing the pacer to lose his stride, in order to avoid bumping Cobweb, which he did anyway, just before reaching the wire.

For all the jostling and rustiness of this opening trial, Dan Patch still broke his own state and track record, posting 1:59 ½—the first sub-two-minute mile in Minnesota harness racing history.

According to one newspaper account, "the crowd broke forth in a burst of applause that would have overpowered a mere czar or emperor." But despite the obvious display of speed, something about the messiness of the race only whetted the appetite for all those fans who had just seen Dan Patch.

"Every one of the thousands who watched him wanted to see the pacer go once more," wrote reporter Frank Force in the *Minneapolis Tribune,* the day after the race. "They knew that the track was slow and heavy and that Dan had really not approached his form ... His pacemakers, too, had kept him back a bit and there was a general feeling that the horse had not had a fair chance to exert himself under the conditions."

There was an immediate plea to the State Fair Board to fix things so that they could get to see Dan Patch again. What made that possibility all the more real was the fact that Dan stayed on at the fair the day after his race stabling in the grounds' barns and working out with Hersey.

Talking to reporters at the state fair track, Hersey hinted that the horse might be willing to go again and observed that he had never seen Dan feeling so fine after a fast mile. Frank Force, who was among the crew watching Dan Patch work out, wrote that "The big pacer cavorted playfully about the track and could only be restrained from attempts at speed with difficulty."

"Minnesota people do not get the chance to see Dan Patch every day in the year," Force went on, "And now that he is at the track, ready to go, they would like to see him as much as possible. ... He has come to be regarded as a Minneapolis horse, but people all over the state have shown great interest in him as was evidenced by the crowd of Monday. Mr. Savage simply stated yesterday that he was willing to allow Dan to appear a second time. It is now up to the state fair men."[2]

With that splendid opening day payout filling his pockets, it was probably a lot easier for M. W. Savage to feel magnanimous toward the Minnesota State Fair. Advocate and promoter of the state that he was, Savage no doubt also wanted to see Dan Patch perform at his very best in Minnesota. But the clincher for a second exhibition for Dan was the fact that the State Fair Board decided to put up a $10,000 prize if Dan broke his own world record of 1:56 for the mile.

So it was agreed that Dan Patch would race again on Saturday, the last day of the fair, and according to newspaper accounts, orders were given by Savage to Hersey that Dan was to be driven to his limit. As a consequence, "[the horse] will probably give an exhibition such as never before seen on any track in the world."

That Saturday an enormous crowd filled every available inch of the grandstands, bleachers, and paddock, with many more crowding up hills at the foot of the track. In the grandstands, spectators went looking everywhere for ways to boost their elevation, so that they could better see the horse. They corralled chairs, pulled stools out from under ticket sellers, and also swiped pop crates and other boxes. One stout woman in a white dress, standing on a barrel, got so excited when Dan came out for his first spin that she started to dance in her Cuban heel shoes on the barrel head. The barrel collapsed and the lady in white disappeared within.

For all the crowding in the stands and around the track, however, attendance for the day was down considerably from the opening on Monday. Gate receipts for this last day of the fair would number around 34,000, a substantial improvement from Saturday's fair gate the year before, but nowhere near the record set on the previous Monday.

Once again, Dan made his first appearance around 2 p.m. and did a jog around the track. A second warm-up an hour and a half later was performed before a capacity crowd, but it would be another hour before Dan made his go at the record.

Once again, Cobweb and a horse named Trolley were serving as Dan's pacers. There wasn't much wind and hopes were high, but a record-breaking run was not to be. Dan did the first quarter in :29 ½. He did a :29 flat in the second quarter, but slowed a bit in the third to :30 ½. His final quarter was a great :28 ½ , but the mile total of 1:57 ½ was a second and a half off his own world record.

If anyone in the Minnesota crowd was disappointed, their long faces were not reported. In fact, according to Force in the *Minneapolis Tribune*, most attendees were made incredulous by Dan's running. "When the time was announced," he wrote, "a large number of the wise ones were inclined to shake their heads, as they did not believe any horse could make the Hamline track in that time."

Local writers were largely an uncritical audience of Dan Patch throughout his career, and the common feeling was that the Hamline track was simply not of the quality of the fast tracks on the Grand Circuit, particularly in Memphis and Lexington. If and when Dan topped his own mark, went the thinking of the racing "wise ones," it would be in one of these venues rather than on his home turf.

In any case, there had been more than enough stardom in Dan's local performances to satisfy his audience. Never before had a horse paced under two minutes in the state, and Dan Patch had done the feat twice in a single week. These were Dan's first two outings of the season, and it was hard to imagine any horse at any time matching the peerless ability of this stallion to step out onto a track and perform in such championship fashion so early in the horse-racing year.

## Warming Up

Just four days after his second run at the Hamline, Dan ran an unpaced mile on a wet track before a record crowd at the Indiana State Fair. With 55,000 fans in his home state cheering him on, Dan ran a respectable 2:00 ½.

The Allentown crowd

In Allentown, Pennsylvania, Dan had another remarkable day at the track. A massive fair crowd of 82,000 people turned out to watch the stallion negotiate Allentown's half-mile track, which he did in a record time of 2:01, breaking his own mark for the mile run on a half-mile track by a full two seconds. His stumbling run the year before in Oklahoma City, with its miraculous recovery, remained a remarkable feat, but it was no longer the record.

Just forty minutes after that first turn, Dan Patch was hitched to a wagon, and once again he broke one of his own records, this one for racing a mile on a half-mile track, to wagon. His time was 2:05, and when he finished the last race, Hersey was picked up and carried into the judges' stand, while throngs of people continued to crowd around, trying to get near the wonderful pacer.[3]

In his first four racing exhibitions of the 1905 season, Dan Patch had been seen by almost 240,000 racing fans, and it is likely that the vast majority of them thought they had just seen the most wonderful harness horse the world had ever produced.

More brilliance was to come. At Chicago, Dan made a run of 2:01 ½ on a half-mile track in wet weather—a mere half-second off the world mark he'd just set in Allentown nine days earlier.

The Patch entourage arrived in the horse racing capital of the country just four days after the Chicago exhibition, and it was here, at Lexington, Kentucky, that Dan would win the lasting applause of the nation's most knowledgeable racing fans.

## "Praise Indeed"

Lexington hosted an annual harness racing event called the Kentucky Breeder's Race that brought almost all of the sports top horses to the city each October.

Dan Patch had first raced in Kentucky as a green five-year-old in 1901, just a year after his debut in the county fair circuit of Indiana. In the Bluegrass State, the son of Joe Patchen had impressed veteran observers by winning three out of three heats with a 2:05 best time.

His next appearance at the Lexington track was 1903, when he had already surpassed all other pacers on the circuit and was as well-known as any harness horse in the country. That year he began a season of remarkable record-breaking runs by pacing a 1:59 ½ to wagon.

Now back for his third go-round at the Breeder's Association Track, Dan was primed for a run at his own mile record.

There were few tracks more conducive to the cause. The Breeder's Track was considered (along with Memphis) one of the two best in the country, and its race crowd as knowledgeable as any in the land. They were, according to a writer for the *Kentucky Farmer and Breeder*, "horse lovers everyone ... appreciative of all the sport offered, and ready to give witness by their plaudits to the credit which the mighty Dan Patch deserved." [4]

On October 5 Dan took to the track for an initial go at the record. It was a Thursday afternoon, conditions were good, the track was fast, and Dan had a great run. In fact, his 1:56 time tied the world record. Rarely has such a remarkable feat been so quickly forgotten. For just two days later, Dan was back on the oval for another go at the clock under cloudless skies and before a crowd that sensed that something special was about to happen. "Conditions could not have been more favorable," said the *Kentucky Farmer and Breeder*, "and the opinion was very general that unless Dan Patch broke his record [that] Saturday he never would."

Scott Hudson and Charley Dean were driving the pace horses, and after the usually preliminary warm-ups around 4:30, the two of them moved in to form a tight huddle around Dan Patch and Harry Hersey. The squadron of horses and sulkies neared the straight away heading toward the start line on the fly—Hudson in front, and Dean to the side. Both were dressed in bright red colors, a habit the Dan Patch racing team had assumed earlier that year to help make a vivid contrast with Hersey, who wore his usual white. Just passed the wire, the trio broke off the start. The same thing would happen again. And once more before they were off.

"Three times they scored down the stretch," went the story in the *Kentucky Farmer and Breeder*, "a runner in front and another at the side." And each time Hersey broke it off, until finally he felt his horse was ready on the fourth trip toward the wire. It was on this pass that Hersey nodded his head, indicating to the timers that the contest was on and suddenly, a strange quiet fell over the grounds. "At no other time during the afternoon was there such perfect silence in the grandstand, and at no other time on any track was interest ever more intense."

It was not a particularly good start, according to the *Lexington Leader*. The starter yelled to Hersey, "Are you ready?" which made Hudson turn to see if Hersey was nodding. In the act, the pacemaker swerved slightly and Dan was momentarily checked, which made for a clumsy beginning. The first quarter ticked off in 29 ½ seconds—not an auspicious start for what was hoped would be a record-breaking run.

By the time the quarter pole was reached, however, "the great brown had gotten into good working order, with that smooth, frictionless action that knows no check and that tolerates no interference ... he began to move in a manner that indicated mighty possibilities," wrote the *Farmer and Breeder*.

According to the *New York Times*, at the first quarter, "Patch's nose was almost against Hudson's coat, and the crowd began vainly yelling to Hudson to move up."

With Dan remaining tight against his pace-setter, the second quarter passed in a blistering 28 seconds—a 1:52 pace for the mile—and the crowd's enthusiasm was rampant. Round the turn in the third quarter, the pacemakers were whipped to greater speed and Dan Patch followed directly on their heels.

The third-quarter time of 1:26 ¼ was flashed out amid wild cheering and frantic yells of "Come on, Dan!" "Come on, Dan!" "You can do it!"

"Men, women, children, all cheered, clapped their hands and called to the horse as he came forward in his mighty effort," said the *Kentucky Farmer and Breeder*, "begging him to accelerate his pace, begging him to survive the killing clip he had set, begging him to break his own record."

Into the stretch went the great pacer, still keeping his even, seemingly effortless stride. According to the *New York Times* report, "the runner at his sulky wheel began to crawl up. Hudson [in the lead] gave a little more rein, but Hersey sat like a statue, not urging his charge with whip or word."

"Now came a splendid race for the wire," wrote the *Lexington Leader*, with Dan "plunging like an engine in a mad race." As he flashed beneath the wire, the crowd in and around the grandstand stood and with bated breath awaited the posting. A deep silence fell over the grounds until the official timekeepers hung up the magical numbers for all to see. They read 1:55 ¼. Dan Patch had just broken his own world's record for pacing a mile.

"Thousands of shouts rent the air," wrote the *Lexington Leader*. "Cheer after cheer was given and when the horse was led back to the judge's stand scenes of unrivaled enthusiasm were enacted."

The *Kentucky Farmer and Breeder* remembered it slightly differently. There was no profound silence and bated breath as the crowd waited for the time to be posted; it was only triumph and noise from the end of the race onward: "They cheered before the time was flashed, they cheered, shouted and cheered when the horse came back to the stand, and they cheered when he was led around three or four times after being unhitched from the sulky ... Men by the hundreds flocked through the gate onto the track that they might pat his silken coat, thus giving one more and one deeper tribute to a record which now knows no counterpart in all the annals of racing."

It was not possible for the police at the gates to stop the crowd from rushing forward, said the reporter. Indeed, "had it been possible in any way to pick Dan Patch up and carry him on their shoulders before the exultant thousands they would have done it." Denied that possibility, "they contented themselves by patting his silken coat, caressing him, by paying him a tribute that he deserved, giving him an ovation that his kind never knew before."

To receive this kind of praise from Kentuckians meant a great deal to Savage, because, as one journalist put it, "Kentuckians are better judges of horses than any other people that live; they have witnessed for years greater contests than can be seen at any other trotting track in the world; equine praise from them is praise indeed."

## All the Records Fit to be Broken

To put Dan Patch's accomplishment into perspective, it may be useful to consider that in approximately one hundred years of harness racing history in the United States, from around 1800 to 1902, just one horse, Star Pointer, had paced or trotted a mile in less than two minutes. From

1902 through his record-breaking run at Lexington in 1905, Dan Patch had accomplished the feat eleven times.

Not only that, he had now set and broken his own mile record five times in less than four seasons of trial racing. In addition, he held and had broken his own records for the fastest miles on a half-mile track, for racing a mile to wagon, for racing a half-mile to sulky, a half-mile to wagon, and for racing two miles.

Dan Patch Puts on a New Crown at Lexington
(From Horse World)

Now Dan had taken the mile record down almost a full second from his previous mark. He had lopped nearly five seconds off that two-minute-mile barrier, and there was no horse, pacer or trotter, in the country who could race with him.

"Sum it all up," wrote the *Lexington Leader*, "and it must be conceded that it was the greatest mile ever paced; that it was paced by the greatest horse that ever stepped around the oval; that it was done on the greatest trotting track in the world and in the presence of one of the greatest crowds of enthusiastic people that ever saw a race meeting in Kentucky."

And what did it matter that for this run, and every other one of his record-setting paces, Dan had employed a front runner, with a dirt shield beneath its sulky? What did it matter that the American Trotting Association had slapped asterisks beside each and every one of those numbers in the record books?

Not only was this a non-issue for the majority of harness racing fans watching Dan Patch, they actually reveled in the excitement generated by Dan's "helpers" on the track. "After the front pace-maker had been legislated out of legality," John Hersey would write later, "Mr. Savage continued to the end to use one in all Dan's exhibitions because in that way the horse could go a faster mile—and because the crowds loved it ... ."

With three and sometimes four horses thundering down the stretch and Dan Patch tight behind the lead runner, an exhibition against time took on the appearance of a thrilling race, even if the only real opponent was the stopwatch. Harness fans lapped up the show. They came out in the tens of thousands to see it.

"Everywhere he appeared, crowds thronged to see him," wrote historian Dwight Akers. "His performances were managed with perfect showmanship ... Dan Patch's trials of speed ... were made vastly exciting by the elaborate preparation expended upon them and by their dramatic execution. Not one but three runners went with him, a horse before him, a horse beside him, and horse behind. It was a field of four with that marvel of energy, the son of 'Old Joe' Patchen, at dead center—a little system of planets circling through space with Dan as its blazing sun riveting all eyes. No wonder that 'Dan Patch Day' on every race course where the brown pacer appeared packed the stands." [5]

There was also the fact, as John Hervey wrote years later, "that he never disappointed them, but could always be counted on to do something grand."

Even so, there were some who, as much as they might have admired Dan Patch, couldn't keep the asterisks out of their heads. It mattered to the record-keepers, trotting officials and, obviously, to Will Savage himself that Dan raced so often with a front-running pace horse carrying a dirt shield. In fact, Savage was about to prove his own concern and sensitivity to the issue.

Just a few days after Dan's record run in Lexington, Savage took the time from the horse's exhibition schedule in Toronto to wire the *Minneapolis Journal*. He wanted to correct a story the paper had done regarding Dan's race in Kentucky. "In your excellent report of his wonderful mile in 1:55 ¼ at Lexington on October 7, it is stated that Dan Patch made his mile behind a wind shield," Savage wrote. "The party in Lexington, who telegraphed this report, must have known it was absolutely false. Dan Patch never used a wind shield in any of his miles ... Only one horse [Prince Alert] ever used a wind shield, and his record was not allowed. I certainly would not be foolish enough to try for records in a way that would not give Dan an official record.

"The trotting association ruled over two years ago that a wind-shield record would be allowed, and at the same time ruled that a small dirt shield under the seat of the sulky to which the pacemaker was hitched would be allowed as a protection from the dirt thrown by the runner in front.

"As Dan Patch is a Minnesota horse, I feel sure you will gladly publish these statements in order that the friends of Dan may know that he is making his wonderful records in an honorable way."

Of course, there was a small measure of ingenuousness about this note. In venting to the local paper, Savage didn't mention the fact that each and every record mile that Dan had run to date was accompanied, in the record book, by a mark questioning its legitimacy. Never mind the distinctions between a dirtshield, a windshield, or an "auto-trotto-yachtic" sail. What about the very presence of a front-runner in these record-setting exhibitions?

No doubt these matters were on Savage's mind even before the record run at Lexington. In fact, at the very end of Dan's victory celebration in Kentucky on October 7, just moments after his record-setting race, he had the track announcer let the crowd know that come Wednesday, the last day of the meet, Dan was going to be back out on the Lexington track. He was going to run without a front runner, without a dirt-shield.

In M. W. Savage's estimation, it was time to remove any lingering doubt about the merits of his horse. He was bound and determined to show that Dan Patch was unmatched in any type of race against time. With or without a frontrunner, Dan Patch was the fastest pacer the world had ever seen.

He wasn't able to prove it at Lexington, however. The weather turned cold and rainy the day after his 1:55 ¼ and stayed that way, with an added wind, through the rest of the week. Come Wednesday, Dan was able to tie the mark of Star Pointer, 1:59 ¼, set way back in 1897. It was his first sub-two-minute mile raced without aid of a lead pacer, and Hersey, Scott Hudson, and the third driver, Charley Dean, declared it one of Dan's greatest miles, but it was impossible not to be disappointed in the outcome.

## Toronto

Toronto, the next stop on Dan's tour, had originally been scheduled as the last leg of his fall tour, but plans to change the date of his season's finale were already in the works. The Canadian track was a half-mile oval—no chance to challenge the unpaced mile record there—and when Patch arrived in mid-October, the weather was once again cold, wet, and raw.

There were distractions as well. First came a story out of Sioux City, Iowa, that the former owner of Joe Patchen, a man named Colonel J. G. Taylor, had proof that Patchen was not actually the sire of Dan Patch; another horse of his named Domineer was really the one who had been matched with Dan's mother Zelica.

From Minneapolis, Savage's brother-in-law, Edward Forester, speaking on his behalf, told reporters that the Patch camp would look into the matter. "Horse lovers," it was concluded in the story, "say it doesn't make any difference to Dan, as he is in a class by himself."

Just as the question on Dan's father was being raised, however, a farmer from Port Arthur, Ontario, was traveling the eight-hundred and fifty miles to Toronto to raise an even more radical issue concerning Dan's true parentage. John Thompson claimed that in the fall of 1896, he'd placed a trotter of his named Arrin in the care of famed driver W. B. Ketcham at a stable near Toronto. On New Year's Eve of that year, the stables burned to the ground, and Thompson's horse disappeared. "It was said that Arrin was destroyed, but afterward other articles announced to have been burned were discovered to have been sold." Now Mr. Thompson had the idea that Dan Patch was actually his missing horse, and after arriving in Toronto and seeing the champion stallion at the track, he was more certain then ever. "If it meant eternity to me," he said. "I could swear Patch is Arrin."

The matter was quickly settled when Hersey brought in a veterinarian who declared that Dan couldn't be fifteen years old, as he would have to have been, according to Thompson's claim. That was to say nothing about the question of how a mediocre trotter could become the fastest pacer in history in a few year's time. Thompson was later thrown out of Dan's stable when a groomsman caught him in the act of examining the horse.

The final distraction provided M. W. Savage the opportunity of using his "Dan Patch is now a good Methodist" line, as he had the year before in St. Louis. The Toronto Driving Club, which was sponsoring the harness race exhibition, had gotten in trouble with the publicly-owned Toronto track where the race was to be held for allowing gambling and the sale of liquor on the site. The Toronto Board of Control, which ran the track, was threatening to pull the license of the Driving Club unless it quit the betting and booze. In lining up on the side of the Board of Control, Savage was able repeat his declaration that his horse was a good Methodist and would never appear anywhere where liquor was served and gambling allowed.

The Toronto Driving Club refrained from its bad habits, and the exhibition was held on a muddy track on a wet October day before five thousand shivering people. Dan ran a 2:06 mile on the half-mile track, lowering the Canadian record by some three seconds.

## Memphis

There was one final drama that season, and it came at a familiar venue for Dan. There had originally been no plan to ship the stallion to Memphis for end of the season exhibitions, but that was before breaking the record for an unpaced mile became a priority for Will Savage. From Toronto, the great stallion went south with one purpose in mind: to beat the 1:59 ¼ record, which he'd already tied at Lexington.

Dan arrived in Memphis in the last week of October, and took his first run at the record on November 1. He made a 2:00 even mile, and followed that up two days later with another record-tying run of 1:59 ¼.

Rain came for the next few days, and Hersey wrote Savage, who was back in Minneapolis attending to business, that he was becoming doubtful about whether or not the weather would cooperate enough to make another run at the record possible for 1905. Hersey received a quick response from his boss intimating that if he planned to spend the winter in Minnesota he had better beat the record first. Thankfully for all involved, the weather broke by November 8 so that Dan was able to make another effort, but again he fell short of the record, pacing the mile in 2:00.

Harness experts had questioned Savage's horsemanship in the past and would do so again in the future, and it was moments like these— forcing his champion to do all of this speedwork so late in the season— that caught their attention. But it was obvious that Savage and the Patch camp were in the grip of an obsession. And they had their supporters, too. "Fish" Jones, writing in the *Horseman and Stockman*, argued that it was necessary to work the horse when he was in prime condition. "All experiences ... show how almost impossible it is to keep a horse at the feather-edge of his extreme flight of speed for any appreciable length of time. Ergo, Dan Patch went to Memphis to fight an uphill fight with the chances of winning new laurels against him."

On November 11, after working several slow miles early in the afternoon, Dan was brought back to the track at 4 p.m. The weather, the track, and the condition of the horse were all perfect.

The crowd was sparse, however. Dan's trials were not being held in the midst of a week of racing events or a fair. The Memphis Cup races had ended a couple of weeks earlier, so these runs were being conducted at the track as a special "Dan Patch" meeting. All the same, Savage and Hersey were careful to meet the requirements laid down by the Trotting Association for performances. That meant that the trials were advertised, admission was charged, at least two other races were conducted on the track that day, and a full contingent of both timers and judges (three of each) was on hand to oversee the exhibition.

Though he had no frontrunners for the go, Dan was to be side-paced once again by his friend Cobweb, driven by Charley Dean. A third horse, driven by R.E. Nails, would trail. In sharp contrast to his previous record-breaking performances, there were not thousands to cheer him on; no crowds to holler as he passed the first quarter in 30 seconds and the half in :59.

Nor were the reporters watching the exhibition particularly impressed: "… :59 for the half mile did not necessarily mean much," wrote the *Trotter and Pacer*, "for Dan Patch had done that before." When he did the three-quarters in :29 ¼, however, "the crowd began to get interested. At that point, Dan Patch had :30 ¾ ahead of him, if he wanted to stay and beat the record."

According to the *Trotter and Pacer*, "There was never a flutter … as the big horse whirled around the last turn." He was a bit wide on the stretch, "waver[ed] just short of the stretch, where he all but made a break" but then he steadied "and finished out in grand style with a new world's record to his credit."

There were no throngs to descend upon the track at the end of Dan's magnificent performance, as had happened so often in the past, but for harness-racing purists and those like his owner and driver who felt compelled to prove Dan's supremacy in every facet of the sport, this 1:58 mile was as important as any he'd ever run.

Jones in the *Horseman and Stockman* could not "refrain from complimenting as well as congratulating Mr. Savage. Many men, indeed most men," he wrote, "would have long since retired Dan Patch from the track." Not M. W. Savage. According to Jones, "Mr. Savage … had much to lose and little to gain by sending his horse against the hardest of all competitors, old Father Time, this year. But he ventured all and has gained all."

As for the horse: "There are no new worlds for Dan Patch to conquer. The Alexander of the horse world, may now rest with all his honors thick upon him, and wait for the time when his sons and daughters will add new luster to the name of Dan Patch."

But it was not up to "Fish" Jones to determine just where and when Dan Patch would race his last. There would be more days at the track to come, and one more record-breaking performance, but what Jones sensed was true. There was no one, not even Old Father Time, challenging Dan Patch any longer.

# 13

# The Franchise

One of the principal reasons for Dan Patch's October 1905 visit to Toronto was to help promote a newly created branch of M. W. Savage's stock food business in Canada. Called the International Stock Food Company, Limited, Savage had organized the division in late 1903 and sent his twenty-year old son, Erle, to Toronto to head the new entity.

This international extension of Savage's Minneapolis business was quickly successful and like its parent was expanded into new more expansive quarters soon after it opened. The Toronto firm was located in a modern, four-story, fireproof, brick building with thousands of square feet of floor space. This branch of the stock food company was soon overseeing not only Canadian operations, but all of the business's international trade, which included stock food shipments to South Africa, the West Indies, and Australia.

At the time International Stock Food and its chief promotional tool, Dan Patch, were as famous in Canada as they were in the United States. "There is practically no hamlet or village in Canada where the name 'International' is not well and favorably known," wrote a Minneapolis business publication in 1907. "From coast to coast the preparations sent out by the company enjoy a large and ever-increasing sale … it is safe to say that the renown of Dan Patch is as well known throughout Canada as it ever was in the United States, due in a great measure to the circulation in every part of the country of literature and reproductions of the famous pacer whose history is so closely linked with that of the International Stock Food Company of Minneapolis."

Like the Minneapolis business, International Stock Food, Limited produced livestock supplements and veterinary supplies and tonics, and also distributed a slew of catalogues and educational literature geared to an international farm audience, published in Minneapolis under the name Illuminated World Life. These publications, along with the original International Stock Food catalogue, a briefly published journal called *Savage's Magazine*, and the numerous Dan Patch lithographs, stock books, and other pamphlets, made Savage's Earth Publishing Company one of the largest publishers in the Twin Cities.

In May of 1906 Savage announced plans to continue his company's expansion. A new plant was to be erected in Minneapolis to produce an innovative variety of stock food made of a mixture of sugar and grains. The idea was to produce a "scientific feed," as the *Minneapolis Journal* described it, "not medicinal, but a ration, having the proper quantities of protein and fat, with a percentage of sugar." Savage's chemists had come up with such a formula, according to the report, and its carefully measured proportions would, they claimed, reduce the cost of fattening stock considerably. Construction on the manufacturing facility in Minneapolis was to commence before the year was out. This new business would be organized as the International Sugar Feed Company and would soon include a plant in Memphis, Tennessee (1909), as well as Minneapolis.

At the same time, Savage was purchasing a number of small manufacturing interests in the Midwest. In one fashion or another, all of these companies were in the business of producing tools and implements that would be useful to a rural, self-sufficient economy. These factories included makers of manure spreaders, sewing machines, thermometers, gasoline engines, watches, knives, washing machines, and incubators for chicken eggs.

Along with the manufacturing items and his ongoing and extensive line of livestock feed products, the Savage companies also included a Dr. Belding Company, which consisted of a line of patent medicines and "toilet preparations" for human consumption which harkened back to M. W. Savage's early business career in Iowa. There were skin remedies for eczema and Dr. Belding Six Prairie Herbs for coughs and cold ("contains no Opium, Morphine, Chloroform, nor any other injurious ingredient"). Dr. Belding also had a remedy for piles and tablets for dyspepsia, as well as a Dr. Belding Tooth Powder and Dr. Belding Wild Cherry Sarsaparilla. There was also a product described in brochures as "a Vegetable tonic and Blood Purifier for men and women worn out by hard work and cares of life."

In addition, the Savage business empire included a food distributorship, and the "M. W. Savage Art Company," which took advantage of the company's colored printing capabilities to distribute mass-market lithographic art prints, which were a rarity. One of the reasons why Dan Patch's image was such a popular farm home adornment was that there were so few alternatives.

Late in 1906 M. W. Savage purchased a well-known traveling circus, the Gentry Brothers' Dog and Pony Shows. Just as its name suggests, this was a troupe which featured performing dogs and ponies (along with some elephants and camels) and catered primarily to an audience of young people. The modern connotation of a "dog-and-pony show"—meaning an overblown sideshow or media campaign—was just coming into being in Savage's day, but the Gentry Brothers' shows were by all accounts quality performances.

Even so, Savage was quick to change the name of the circus to the "Gentry Brothers Trained Animal Shows." He was also quick to promote its menagerie as the latest beneficiaries of the wonders of his

International Stock Food Tonic. Savage felt no compunction about printing a letter from the manager of the Gentry Brothers Trained Animal Shows, Mr. I. G. Speers, in *The Racing Life of Dan Patch 1:55*, which endorsed both the Tonic and the company's "Silver Pine Healing Oil." Never mind that Speers was in the employ of Savage: "Everywhere we appeared," wrote Speers to Savage, "the magnificent appearance of our stock excited universal interest and comment. . . We attribute the above success to the daily use of your splendid stock food tonic which did wonders for us ... We even administered your stock food tonic occasionally to our elephants, four camels and other hay-eating animals, with very beneficial results." [1]

For a time in 1910 Savage would also briefly join the fledgling automobile market when he purchased the entire factory output of an Indiana manufacturer—1500 cars. These vehicles included 2-cylinder "runabouts" priced from $475 to $750; a two-seated roadster, going at $1,400; a five-seated, four-cylinder passenger car for $1,850; and two- and four-ton trucks, priced to move at $1,000 for the former and $1,250 for the latter.

M. W. Savage's son Erle, who by this time was splitting his workload between Toronto and Minneapolis, was slated to manage this latest enterprise, though in an article announcing the business in the *Minneapolis Tribune*, it was stated that both Savages "are experienced motor car owners and drivers and the selection of the new line was based on their experience with many makes of cars in their own garages."

To this dizzying array of tools and implements, medicines, and printwork, the Savage companies attached the name and image of their familiar icon, Dan Patch. Farm families throughout the world could conveniently purchase any or all of it simply by placing an order through the ever-expanding International Stock Food Catalogues. Taking advantage of the Twin Cities status as a railroad-shipping hub, M. W. Savage was creating a broad-based mail order business that was beginning to resemble, though it could not rival, the giant Sears and Roebuck.

In 1911 all of the enterprises including the original International Stock Food Company were folded into one giant firm called M. W. Savage Factories, Incorporated, for which Savage claimed to have a mailing list of 2.5 million farm families.[2]

The company was run by a small coterie of men with son Erle filling the role of right-hand man to his father. Erle was said to have organized the M. W. Savage Factories and would ultimately serve as its president. Will Savage's second son, Harold, was still a boy through these years of corporate growth. He was most notable for a photo that his

The young Erle Savage

father used frequently in company literature showing eight-year old Harold and some friends riding in a sled pulled by Dan through the streets of Minneapolis in the middle of Dan's first winter in the state. It foreshadowed a lifelong interest in harness racing for Harold—one that Erle apparently never shared.

At the same time, the International Stock Food Factory, still housed at the old Exposition Building on the Mississippi across from the Union Depot, remained the backbone of the M. W. Savage business. It was still the largest company of its kind in the world, employing 700 people, keeping 200 typewriters busy, and handling between two and five thousand letters a day. The largest single office in the world in 1903—675 feet long by 125 feet wide—remained the largest single office in the world in 1911. But Savage's advertising budget had jumped to $300,000 a year.

## Booze Fighters Need Not Apply

Even as Savage was expanding his business enterprises on a host of fronts, he kept a close eye on the development of his International Stock Food Farm, where Dan Patch was joined in the winter of 1906 by another champion horse, Arion, a seventeen-year old trotter from the estate of the recently deceased Malcolm Forbes.

Arion's racing career was long over, but he still held the record for the fastest time by a two-year-old trotter. In 1891, two years after setting the record, he had been sold to Forbes by Governor Leland Stanford of California for a record-setting $125,000. Will Savage had paid considerably less for Arion—$2,500—but the stallion's personal history added to the élan of the farm, which was fast becoming a tourist hotspot in the Minnesota River Valley. No one in the Upper Midwest and few people in the country had ever seen a farm and stable quite like it, and in 1907 plans were developed to make it even more spectacular.

Ground was broken in the fall of that year for the construction for the world's first and only completely enclosed half-mile training track, which would allow for winter-time training for Savage's horses. Designed by Seth Griffin (who had also designed the stables and outdoor track) the indoor facility had a thirty-foot wide oval and was built just to the west of the stables. The turf was covered with salt and tanbark, spread over the black loam of the Minnesota River Valley. Fourteen-hundred windows made every portion of the track  clearly visible, according to the *Minneapolis Journal*, and it was all covered by a wood-framed roof sealed with asbestos.[3]

Ken McCarr grew up near the International Farm, where his father worked as a trainer and driver under Savage in the early 1910s. A half-century later, McCarr would become a turf writer for *Hoofbeats* and tell of his experiences on the farm, including recollections of the indoor track, which was completed in January 1908.

The covered racetrack, wrote McCarr, "was fairly narrow but two horses could jog abreast without crowding." Near the turns, the length of view was limited, said McCarr, and drivers were careful to avoid collision.

The novelty of the indoor oval stayed vivid in his mind: "Years have not erased the sound of the hoofbeats muffled by the tanbark dust that hung in the air even up to the raftered ceiling . . ." During the sub-zero weather, there would be explosive crackings—a sound, the grooms told McCarr, caused by the frost "squeezing the nails up in those rafters."[4]

In the summertime, McCarr remembered, "the mares and foals were turned out in big pastures that extended along the banks of the Minnesota river. Passengers on the main train line always had a good chance to see horses as the train ran about 100 yards in front of the big barn and skirted the pastures for some distance.

"The inevitable brook wandered through the farm. It passed close by the big barn near the three springs enclosed by concrete walls, spring water so pure that it was bottled and sold . . ."

Fishing for suckers, catfish, and carp was a frequent pastime at the farm, and McCarr's reminiscences are accompanied by a photo of himself as a seven-year old boy standing beside an eighty-two pound catfish caught on the property by the farm's blacksmith.

Aside from the brooks and springs, there was a nearby pond that served as a wintertime training ground for a unique form of harness racing—ice races, which were held on Minneapolis' Lake of the Isles and at the St. Paul Winter Carnival for several decades extending from the 1890s into the 1930s. Savage's International Stock Food Farm sent a number of its horses to these competitions, including one of its best pacers, George Gano, but Dan Patch was never asked to race on the ice.

Gano was part of a string of talented standardbreds whom Savage purchased and brought to the farm as Dan Patch's career began to wane. Among them was Cresceus, the same gifted trotter who'd been the star attraction at Brighton Beach way back in 1901 when Dan Patch made his first appearance in New York (Savage paid $21,000 for him in early 1906 and would ultimately sell him to a Russian buyer for $25,000 in the spring of 1908). Also among Savage's stable were Hedgewood Boy (2:01); Lady Maud C, a mare, who owned her gender's world record for the half-mile; and perhaps the most talented of his buys, Minor Heir (1:58 ½), who cost M. W. Savage $40,000 in the winter sale of 1908 and would achieve the most notable career after Dan Patch's of the International Farm stable.

In addition, Dan Patch sired and the farm trained scores of his offspring, including the talented Dazzle Patch, who once did a :56 ¾ half mile. Of all Dan's children, Dazzle Patch was thought to have the best chance of matching his father's gifts, but there was a long list of Patch "children" who would ultimately race in 2:30 or better.

The International Stock Food Farm drew guests from all over the world to view this cavalcade of horseflesh, including H. H. Topakyan, a Persian consul general to the United States, whose base of operations in this country was New York. Topakyan stayed with M. W. Savage at Savage's Valley View home in Bloomington overlooking the farm during his visit to Minnesota. He offered this testimonial, which his host was happy to print in *The Racing Life of Dan Patch 1:55*: "I visited a large number of stock farms in the East, and I have bought some horses from near Lexington, Kentucky. The people of these sections seem to think they have the only stock farms. If they could see Mr. Savage's plant they would have their opinions changed. Minnesota and the Northwest should be proud of an institution like this one, which is sure to have a big effect upon the harness horse breeding industry of the United States and the world." [5]

Other observers were impressed by the atmosphere of the farm, "the air of comfort and well being that pervades the place. The colts and horses are thrifty, well fed and contented. The men, of whom there are a large number, are courteous, cheerful and competent. There is no friction or fussing; every man knows exactly what to do and does it. It is a good place to work … good and clean men are sought. No booze fighters need apply."

But even with all of the talented standardbreds, the well-kept nature of the place, its good fishing and unique structures, the main attraction of the International Stock Food Farm remained Dan Patch, who after many years of cross-country travel and strenuous racing remained the same good-natured, even-tempered individual that he had been during his early years in Indiana.

One visitor to the farm noted that Dan remained as he'd always been, "a horse of sturdy, powerful build, yet fine and clean. His head is beautiful and his eyes reflect his perfect disposition."

Interior and exterior of Valley View

A single look suggested his gifts, thought this visitor. His neck ran gracefully into thick-muscled shoulders. His back was strong and streamed into rear quarters as muscular as his front. He was, simply, "a splendid type of the American harness horse. We have yet to see a cut or photograph that does him even a fair share of justice ... there is an air of greatness and grandeur about Dan that is beyond the power of the camera to delineate."

DAN PATCH 1:55

Grandstand of the Minnesota State Fair following
Dan's record-breaking run, 1906.

# 14

# Dan Patch 1:55

In the late summer of 1906 as Dan Patch began his eleventh year on Earth, his seventh year as a racer, and his fourth year wearing the colors of M. W. Savage, there was nothing that he needed to prove as a racehorse. He was undefeated in fifty-six competitive meets, holder of every major timed record in harness racing history, and he had already eclipsed the magic two-minute mark more times than all other pacers and trotters combined.

On the other hand, as the 1906 racing season opened he could still pace faster than any horse in the country, and thousands of people were still willing to pay to see him do it. Will Savage saw no reason to deny them the opportunity. Thoughts of the horse's retirement may have been in the back of his mind, but Savage was not ready to send Dan Patch out to pasture to be viewed by the tourists venturing south from Minneapolis toward the Minnesota River Valley.

That Dan remained in competitive shape was made evident in his first test of the year in Galesburg, Illinois. He broke the Illinois state record for a paced mile that afternoon with a 1:57 ¾ time. Likewise across the Mississippi in Iowa, he broke that state's record for the mile toward the end of August when he raced a 1:58 in M. W. Savage's old stomping ground of Dubuque.

All seemed like business as usual as Dan prepared for his third go of the season at the familiar track of the Minnesota State Fair in Hamline, where expectations for a brilliant performance were as high as they'd been the year before.

## The Champion Returns

Despite this being Dan Patch's third visit to the state fair, his appearance there remained a region-wide event, and Savage set the now-familiar promotional tactics in motion to publicize it. The familiar gamut of fair "types" were out in full force, from the speed addicts of the racetrack to the farmers, the city sharps, and the merely curious.

The weekend before the Monday opening of the fair, visitors flooded into the three depots in Minneapolis: the Union saw twenty thousand arrivals, the Milwaukee handled ten thousand, and the Chicago, Great Western and St. Louis station served ten thousand more. The half-dozen major hotels in downtown Minneapolis were crammed and had to set up an additional 550 cots for guests.

Once again, Dan was scheduled to appear on the opening day of the fair, and once again, the turnstiles clicked as they'd never clicked before. In addition to Dan Patch, the day would feature the opening of a new livestock amphitheater at the fairgrounds, which was to be dedicated by James J. Hill, St. Paul's great railroad builder. The famed trotting champion Cresceus, recently purchased by M. W. Savage, was

# CAN DAN PATCH

## BREAK THE WORLD RECORD?

# SATURDAY P. M.

### (3 TO 4 O'CLOCK)

# AT MINNESOTA STATE FAIR

## SPECIAL NOTICE.

The track will be better, Dan will be faster, and Mr. Savage promises that every possible effort will be made to break the world's record of 1:55¼ on Saturday afternoon. Dan will pace three miles and his fastest mile will be about 4 o'clock. If you want to see a thrilling sight and witness a wonderful performance be sure and visit the great Minnesota State Fair on Saturday.

also on hand and scheduled to precede Dan Patch in an exhibition run against the clock.

In between the horse races, the crowd in the grandstand was to be entertained by Patrick and Francisco, billed as Rube Acrobats, and a Ladies' Relay Riding Race, which featured a trio of young women engaged in a strenuous twenty-four mile race. The Four Picards, billed as The World's Greatest Aerial Bar Performers, and comedians Clayton, Jenkins, and Jasper were also scheduled that day for grandstand entertainment. [1]

The fireworks spectacular that evening was a re-enactment of the burning of Moscow, though one reviewer found it difficult to follow the thread of the story. "By far the best part of the spectacle," he wrote, "comes after the Moscow business is off the boards [when] the fireworks are magnificent, profuse and novel."

By the time James J. Hill stepped to the podium to open the fair and inaugurate the new livestock auditorium at 11 a.m., more than thirty-five thousand visitors had already come streaming through the gates. Even more would arrive before Dan Patch raced at 4 p.m.

Some who were crammed into the brand new auditorium to hear Hill speak may have seen a vein of irony in their circumstances. In his speech Hill warned about the dire circumstances that would face future generations of Americans as the global population increased and natural resources dwindled. Soil was being rapidly depleted by wasteful farming methods, said Hill, and coal and iron resources were being used with a rapaciousness that would spell disaster by 1950, when the population of the nation was predicted to surpass 200 million. And here they stood— as if to prove his point—jammed shoulder-to-shoulder and scarcely able to move.

Hill was nearing the end of a career that had begun in St. Paul almost fifty years earlier. He'd arrived as an eighteen-year-old from Canada and found a job as a clerk for a steamship line. In the course of time he had built the Great Northern Railroad into an industry giant and become one of the nation's wealthiest men.

Hill's railroad stretched from Minnesota to the Pacific through territory peopled with settlers, many of whom had been lured onto the western Minnesota and Dakota plains by the Great Northern itself and had subsequently spent their lives paying the only available rate—Mr. Hill's—to ship their wheat back to Eastern markets. While Hill's lecture was well-received in the press, it was also said to have been hard to hear in the new auditorium—which might have been a kind way of suggesting that some in the audience were reluctant to listen to a conservationist sermon from a man who'd already got more than his share of the wealth from the land. At any rate, several thousand of Hill's would-be listeners drifted away toward the harness races long before The Empire Builder was through, only to meet up with another and much larger standing-room-only audience at the grandstand.

By one o'clock the stands were overflowing with race-goers, and spectators had spilled out on to the hills outside the fence, where they tussled with one another for seats in the grass. Still they came. "The street cars ran onto the loops near the Minneapolis gates just as fast they could be operated," reported the *Minneapolis Journal.* "There was not a cessation of the incoming flow of eager sightseers until late in the afternoon. Not until four o'clock, at which hour it was known that Dan Patch would make his appearance, did the gatemen get even a minute's breathing spell." [2]

The total number of visitors would reach more than 90,000, a figure that supplanted 1905's record gate by 25,000 and represented a six-fold increase from the approximately 16,000 fairgoers who came for opening day festivities in 1904 when Dan Patch didn't race.

It seemed like every one of these fairgoers had crowded the track as Dan's start time neared. After a few preliminary heats with local horses, Dan Patch finally appeared on the raceway for his customary warm-ups. He did a 2:11 mile and returned to the stables, at which time expectations for the day were dampened by track veterans, who proclaimed the oval to be two seconds slow. Comedians and acrobats and more harness races followed one another, as the fans stood around debating whether this would be the day the state of Minnesota would get to see their favorite son break his own world's record for pacing a mile.

Cresceus took his spin around the track, but this was not his crowd. Few applauded his performance and a reporter for the *Tribune* speculated fancifully that the older horse "must be green with envy of Dan Patch."

The crowd favorite made his long-anticipated appearance at four o'clock along with two running mates. The start was a good one, but the first quarter time of :29 ½ was not one for the record books. Neither was the half, which Dan finished in :58 ½. He did a :28 ¾ for the third leg of the mile, and a :29 ¼ through the final turn, but his full time for the mile, 1:56 ½, was off Dan's Lexington mark by a full second and a quarter.

## Dan Patch 1:55

As he had done the previous year after a somewhat disappointing first-race day at the Minnesota State Fair, M. W. Savage quickly decided to let Dan Patch have another go at the record on the Hamline track. No horse but Dan had ever come within two seconds of a 1:56 ½, but by this stage in his career, anything but a record was simply an ordinary performance for the stallion. Within a few days it had been decided that Dan would race once more that coming weekend on the last day of the fair. And this would be a genuine attempt to set the record, not simply an effort by the Fair Board and Will Savage to draw more people to the fair.

"Dan Patch is to go again," announced track writer Frank Force in the *Minneapolis Tribune*. "It is with the belief that Dan can [break the record] that he is to be started. Mr. Savage has a sublime confidence in the ability of his champion. He relies to a great extent on the knowledge given him by Harry Hersey ... [who] while refusing to give any estimate on the speed that Dan might make on Saturday, hinted that Dan was stronger than ever and that the champion pacer would better his state record, should he appear again."

Fair officials, too, were guaranteeing a quality race against time. "Everything possible has been done to improve the track," wrote Force, "and if it has ever been fast it will be fast on Saturday. Hundreds of men will be employed to put the course in shape and it is probable that on Saturday the Minnesota state fair track will be in the best condition in its history."

Advertisements for the Saturday exhibition were more succinct in assuring fans that they would see something special: "The track will be better, Dan will be faster and Mr. Savage promises that every effort will be made to break [the] world's record of 1:55¼ Saturday afternoon ... If you want to see a thrilling sight and witness a wonderful performance, be sure and visit the great Minnesota State Fair on Saturday."

For all the assurances and hype, the crowd for the exhibition on Saturday was closer to 35,000 than 90,000, a fact that would take on more importance in years to come as the numbers who would claim to be at that track on September 8, 1906 would jump considerably—on a par, perhaps, with those who claimed to have seen Babe Ruth's "called shot" in the 1932 World Series.

Archie McColl, a twenty-one-year-old farmer from Savage, whose family provided hay to the International Stock Food Farm, was almost certainly one of the attendees. At any rate, his story, told to a newspaper reporter almost sixty years after the event, passed the first test of verisimilitude: he had the right day of the week.

"It was a Saturday afternoon, and I took the Omaha train to Saint Paul and then went to the fairgrounds. I got there rather late and found a large crowd gathered around the race track," McColl recalled.

The grandstand was packed and the crowd near the fence was jammed so tight to the rail that McColl couldn't elbow his way to the front, nor could he see over the heads of the crowd in front of him. He improvised:

"There were several boys around with pails which they used to pick up bottles. I asked one of the boys how much he wanted for his bucket. He sold it to me for twenty-five cents. By turning the pail upside down, I could stand on it and look over the crowd of people in front of me. A fellow standing next to me suggested placing a length of board across the top of the pail. That way both of us could make use of the one pail. After that, the boys were doing a good business in selling pails."

Conditions were not great for a record-breaking run early in the afternoon. The track was fast after a thorough wetting down on Friday night, and caretakers scoured the surface for stray pebbles, scraps of paper, or any object which might upset the horses. But there was one thing the crew could do nothing about: a stiff breeze was blowing intermittently across the track.

Dan came out for his two o'clock warm-ups and ran an unpaced mile before heading back to the stables.

At three p.m. driver Charley Dean appeared behind Cobweb and then out came Dan Patch once more with Harry Hersey in tow. The two horses warmed up together, and again Dan did a mile, this time paced by Dean driving Cobweb before they all went back to the stables for a final cooling off before their final effort.

But at four o'clock, the scheduled time for the trial, the breeze kicked up again and the race was delayed. The sideshow comedians and acrobats worked hard to amuse the increasingly discontented audience until 4:45 when the wind appeared to let up, and Charley Dean returned to the track, this time with two more pacers. They were R. E. Nash, who doubled as the blacksmith at the International Stock Food Farm, driving Trolley on Dan Patch's flank, and Barney Barnes, driving a horse named Peggy O'Neill, who would wait at the half-mile post to drive the horses toward the finish line. Cobweb was to lead the parade with Dean behind him on a sulky that carried the familiar dirt shield that would prevent turf from kicking up on Dan Patch.

By the time the champion pacer came out for his run, the track had been scraped repeatedly until its surface was hard and fast. After all the deliberations of the afternoon, the next few moments passed with lightning speed. The horses went up the stretch, turned, and then thundered back down the straight away with Dan hooked in behind Dean and a runner on his flank. It was only a trial run, and at the turn all four horses eased their pace and jogged down the backstretch. After another practice run Dean had worked his pace horse up to a lather though Dan Patch still looked as if he'd just come from the stall.

Finally Hersey felt his horse was ready, and he notified the judges by raising his whip. The horses and their drivers prepared for the race on the far side of the track, and as the crowd held its breath, Dean suddenly let his runner go and dived into the pole with Hersey deftly sending Dan in behind him. The second runner took the outside and, as the *Pioneer Press* later described it, "the trio came down the stretch in a swirling cloud of dust, a seeming incarnation of the spirit of speed." As the phalanx of horses thundered by the stand the judges started their watches, and the assault on the world's record was on once again.

Dan Patch stayed with his nose against Dean's shoulder, while Dean whipped Cobweb to keep up the pace. Dan was running smoothly from the start, pacing almost like a machine. The lead runner could not shake him off, and the second runner, who was positioned on the outside, was struggling to keep up. According to a St. Paul sports writer named O'Loughlin, "The trio disappeared in a cloud of dust at the first turn to emerge at the quarter with Dan still pacing like a wraith."

The first mark was reached in a blistering :28 ¼, and as they rounded the first bend and began to race away from the grandstand, it was still obvious that Dan was going great guns.

The time for the half was 57 seconds—a 1:54 pace, which put the record in serious jeopardy. On the backstretch Dean let Cobweb go, pulling slightly further ahead of Dan Patch and spurring him on all the more. When they reached the far side of the track, the trio of Dan, Cobweb, and Trolly was joined by Barney Barnes. He was driving Peggy O'Neill, which made four horses and a thick fog of Minnesota topsoil as they headed into the track's far corner.

"The dust clouded behind the flying horses," wrote O'Loughlin. "The sun shone thru the haze of dust and smoke, silhouetting the horses so that they formed the central point of the picture with everything else in the landscape blotted out." As they neared the stretch, the sound of the hoofbeats and the cries of the drivers grew louder as all were aimed now right toward the hosts of cheering fans in the grandstands.

The third quarter had been traveled in :29 ¼—the slowest of the tour to date—and Dan would need to best 29 seconds to break the record. The horses came thundering down the homestretch with Hersey sitting immovable on the white sulky while Dan seemed to be pacing as easily and freely as during the preliminary trials.

The crowd had begun a relentless chant when the split-times suggested the possibility of a record-breaking run, and the roar increased on the home stretch as the horses continued to thunder along. But when Dan passed beneath the wire there were sudden cries for silence. The cheering did abate momentarily, but few in the grandstand found it possible to suppress their feelings for long.

When the announcer finally put a megaphone to his lips to make the call the crowds had been waiting for, the end of his sentence was drowned out in cheers:

"Dan Patch has paced the mile out in 1:55 flat, breaking the world's …"

The fans poured out of the stands onto the track to surround Dan Patch. Meanwhile, Harry Hersey was escorted to the judges' stand for a weigh-in. When everything was pronounced to be in accordance with turf regulations another wild demonstration took place.

M. W. Savage was also called to the judges' stand, and when he was introduced to the audience, he received an ovation only equaled by that of the announcement of the breaking of the record itself.

Cries of "Speech! Speech!" arose from the grandstand, but Savage demurred. "Dan does my speechmaking," he shouted and proceeded to seek out Hersey to give him a hug and congratulations.

Meanwhile, love was heaped on Dan Patch like a thick stack of warming blankets. As he was taken through the throngs back to his stable, a cheering mob accompanied him all the way. Fans and well-wishers lingered around the stables until long after sunset, and they finally had to be driven away so Dan could get some rest.

# The Tribune was there

**Dan Patch and trainer-driver Harry Hersey**

There were 93,000 spectators at the Minnesota State Fair Sept. 8, 1906, when Dan Patch, greatest and most admired of pacers, set a world's mile pacing record.

At the time, more than 60 years ago, the Minneapolis Tribune reported that the horse set the record of one minute and 55 seconds after a two-mile warmup in intense heat.

Wherever a record is set—at the fair, at Metropolitan Stadium or at any other location in the world—you can expect to read about it in detail and depth in the Tribune.

*Experience gained in 100 years of reporting the news—one of many reasons why you benefit from reading the Tribune regularly.*

Minneapolis Tribune
1867 - 1967
**100 YEARS**
OF SERVICE
Centennial

In this Minneapolis Tribune ad, the date is right but the attendance figure is wrong. Only 35,000 saw Dan's record-breaking run that Saturday. 93,000 attended the previous Sunday.

There would be much confusion in later years about just when, where, and how Dan Patch set his final world record in the mile. Much of the dust obscuring the facts was kicked up by Will Savage himself, who would frequently advertise his horse's record run as having been performed before an awesome crowd of ninety-three thousand at the 1906 Minnesota State Fair rather than the thirty to thirty-five thousand spectators who actually attended the Saturday race at the fair.

There would also be a controversy about Dan Patch's record time. The small dirt shield carried by Charley Dean's sulky would be subsequently ruled an illegal windshield by the American Trotting Association, which refused to acknowledge the Hamline time in its record book and kept his low mark at 1:55 ¼ (with an asterisk, because it was conducted using a front pacing horse).

Of course, few in the state of Minnesota, including M. W. Savage himself, cared a whit about the opinion of the American Trotting Association. Nor did it seem terribly important whether the mark had been made on Monday before 93,000 folks or on Saturday before a lesser crowd. The fact of the matter was that Dan Patch had broken his own world's record for pacing a mile on his home track at the Minnesota State Fairgrounds. Now and forever more he was to be Dan Patch 1:55, and no nitpicking collection of killjoys could take that away from him or his adoring fans.

## Into the Future

As early as October 1906, less than a month after Dan's record run at the Minnesota State Fair, M. W. Savage had taken the first of a series of motion pictures of Dan Patch at his exhibition in Springfield, Illinois. He would shoot more movies of Dan in action at the 1907 Minnesota fair, at a 1908 exhibition in Sioux City, Iowa, and in the 1909 season at Sedalia, Missouri. There was also footage shot of Dan and his handlers at the main stable of the stock farm with its famous oriental-looking water tank looming prominent in the background, and of Dan with

Mr. Savage, both looking comfortably familiar with one another, old partners in a successful enterprise.

Always the advertising innovator, Savage had quickly seen the potential of the motion picture as a sales tool. He not only distributed his Dan Patch films to local nickelodeons and theaters for viewing, he also put still images from the film in flipbooks, which he sent to his customers for twenty-five cents a booklet or for simply answering three questions: Where had they seen this offer? How much livestock did they own? And how many acres of land did they farm?

All of this was done with posterity in mind, according to International Stock Food literature: "Fifty years from now or even a hundred years from now these moving picture films will show the world's famous champion, of all champions, in one of his sensational bursts of speed and just as natural and life-like as if Dan [were] actually pacing a mile right before an immense throng of cheering horse admirers."

As with so much of the Dan Patch legend, the story of the film footage would be fudged a little in the telling. Once again, the source of this obfuscation was the advertising of M. W. Savage. Initially, the flipbooks were marketed as images of Dan Patch 1:55 taken at the various racing venues already mentioned. In subsequent editions of the catalog, they became simply images of Dan Patch 1:55. And then at some point, they became images of Dan Patch racing his record-breaking 1:55 at the Minnesota State Fair.

In point of fact only the thirty or thirty-five thousand fans who were at the state fair that day could claim to have seen the magical 1:55. The distinction became more important as the years passed, and it became obvious that Dan Patch would never again break a record on a harness racing track.

Signs of Dan's fading prowess were soon to appear. Just four days after the Hamline race, he performed in Sioux City, Iowa, before a crowd of thirty-five thousand, where he ran an exhibition on a rainy track in 2:02 ½. On September 21 he was back at Allentown, Pennsylvania, where he'd paced magnificently on the fairgrounds half-mile track the year before. He failed to match his world record mark for a mile paced on a half-mile track, however, running 2:05 ½.

In Springfield, Illinois, another familiar venue and the site of his first appearance before the cameras, Dan ran a 1:59 ½. Back at Lexington, where he'd shined so brightly the fall before, Dan ran a 1:58, which seemed rather pedestrian, in light of all he'd done before in Kentucky.

Dan made another unsuccessful attempt to break his own record for the mile in Birmingham, Alabama, and a few weeks later, in Fort Worth, Texas, he hurt an ankle on a poorly-groomed half-mile track, which brought his 1906 season to a premature conclusion.

The 1907 season began with a fairly heavy schedule of exhibitions at Terre Haute, Decatur, and Dubuque. Dan failed to break the two-minute mile in any of these races. He did run a 1:58 ¼ at the Minnesota State Fair on a windy day in Hamline just before the Columbus trip. But it was hard for fans not to notice that a horse who had consistently bested himself and had stayed in remarkably good health through eight years of hard racing—the single exception being the scare in Topeka in 1904—was suddenly looking mortal. In September Dan wrenched an ankle coming from his stable to the track for some exercise in Columbus, Ohio, once again bringing the season to an end prematurely with a mishap.

Savage and Hersey decided to put Dan on a light exhibition schedule in 1908, refusing any venue that might be hazardous to his health. "The champion's energies will not be wasted in going fast miles over poor tracks in bad weather at inopportune times," the *Minneapolis Journal* reported. "His strength and speed will be conserved [for] one mighty effort to establish a new world's record." This effort would be made "at whatever time and place the most perfect conditions exist."

Though this sounded like the schedule of a semi-retired racer, the Dan Patch team was excited by a late August trial run at the farm, made simply for the benefit of a group of reporters gathered to check out Dan's condition and to quiz Savage and Hersey about their limited exhibition season. The twelve-year-old stallion did a 2:00 mile on the Minnesota River bottoms track and looked as fast to the expert eyes watching as he'd ever looked in his life.

Two weeks later he was shipped to Detroit for a run at his record at the Michigan State Fair. The crowd of thirty thousand made the effort more difficult for Hersey by spilling out of the infield onto the track in the middle of the trial. All the same, Dan Patch came through with a 1:58 ⅜, which set a new state record for pacing.

There was just one more try at the world record that year, in Lexington, in the first week of October. Dan made two goes that afternoon. In the first one, he paced a 1:57 ¼. In the second one, he started well, and at the three-quarters pole, he was racing at a 1:25 ½ clip. Anything better than :29 ½ on the final leg would have broken the record. Unfortunately Cobweb, his old partner in exhibition racing, broke a blood vessel in his nose in the last quarter while running ahead of Dan and had to check-up. Dan himself had to slow, too, and all hopes of a record-breaking run vanished in an instant.

Cobweb's driver, Scott Hudson, was asked by Savage to write a testimonial describing how fast Dan Patch was going that day before Cobweb slowed him down. Savage later published the note in *The Racing Life of Dan Patch, 1:55*, as proof that Dan Patch was still a potential record-breaker in 1908.

"There is no doubt in my mind but Dan Patch was faster this fall at Lexington than any time I have ever seen him," Hudson wrote. "In his mile in 1:56 ½, he met with all kinds of bad luck, the runner having started to bleeding at the nose just as he left the half-mile pole. When we reached the three-quarter pole in 1:25 ½, Dan was as full of pace as when we left the wire. After striking me with his nose several times [Hudson was in front of Dan, driving Cobweb], it was necessary to pull Dan up enough to check him, because the runner could not go as fast Dan wanted to pace and yet Dan finished this Wonderful mile in 1:56 ½. I consider this mile the greatest of his life and there is no doubt but what Dan would have beaten his 1:55 record, had not the runner started bleeding at the nose, which caused him to check up in Dan's way." [3]

Hudson's review of the race was no doubt accurate, and M. W. Savage considered it important enough to publish, but such testimonials were starting to sound like an unnecessary rationalization for a failure that was less Dan Patch's than Mother Nature's. After all, this was a twelve-year-old horse who had been racing for eight glorious seasons: Why did Dan Patch need to prove he was faster in 1908 than 1906?

## Homecoming

For any great athlete, the end of a career is difficult to accept. Although the ability to perform with excellence on a continuing basis—the hallmark of great athleticism—is gone, the possibility of one more magical performance lingers. In his prime, Dan Patch had broken so many records over so many years that success had become habitual for him and by extension for his handlers. It was hard for those watching him in his last years to believe that they had already witnessed his last record-breaking run.

In the fall of 1909 Savage and Hersey hauled Dan out for one last season. They paired him with the rising star of the stable, the newcomer Minor Heir, and set him to work in a series of match races. The first event, in Grand Forks on July 20, was memorable because on that occasion Minor Heir became the first and only horse to best Dan in a head-to-head competition.

The two raced again in Springfield, Ohio, in August and then in Sedalia, Missouri, where Dan and Minor Heir were filmed; then came Shreveport, Louisiana, and Phoenix, Arizona. Following the initial loss in North Dakota, Dan Patch bested his rival repeatedly, but Ken McCarr, no doubt repeating the assessment of his International Stock Food trainer father, was doubtful about the legitimacy of the contests: "It was the duty of the younger horse to finish second to the star of the stable in the exhibition miles," he would write in *Hoofbeats* years later.

At Shreveport, Louisiana, Minor Heir was beaten by Dan Patch in 2:09 and then came back later on the same day to go an exhibition mile in 2:02 ¼. After finishing second in 2:03 ¼ at Phoenix, Arizona, Minor Heir came back a few days later and paced in 1:59 ¼. "There is no doubt that old Dan could have handled this pacer in his heyday but Dan was over the hill and Minor Heir was under wraps," wrote McCarr. [4]

Despite the questionable competitiveness of these final exhibitions, and despite the fact that Dan was no longer drawing tens of thousands of spectators, there was still a mystique about him. "Men, women and children seemed content just to see him," said John Hervey, even if they knew he would never break a record again.

Perhaps because he was so busy with other projects, Savage had lately hired a newspaperman named M. E. Harrison as a publicist for Dan Patch. Harrison later wrote a book, *The Autobiography of Dan Patch*, in which he pushed the long-established conceit of putting words into Dan's mouth to an extreme: the entire book was written from the horse's point-of-view.

The *Autobiography* describes a final season filled with travel, exhibitions, and discomforts for Dan. He and his team traveled thirteen thousand miles, during which another injury to his leg hampered his performances. Though the leg improved enough for him to win his final exhibitions, he was obviously not the horse he'd been.

There was a touch of seediness to the end of the season. In Shreveport, some would-be visitors to Dan's stable were turned back by the horse's blacksmith and a pair of attendants. A fight ensued and everyone involved wound up in the hoosegow.

All in all, it was a rather ignoble way to end the last season in the spotlight for harness racing's most magnificent pacer.

Dan Patch did one final mile in Los Angeles, finishing his last racing quarter in thirty seconds on December 4, 1909. According to Harrison, he had a perceptible limp as he was led back to the stands to receive yet another floral offering. "He trembled as he bowed his appreciation when this last of a thousand wreaths was fastened about his shining neck ... as the monarch limped away to the stable, a silence of sadness settled over the crowd and tears glistened in the eyes of many of the spectators as they watched this exit of the noblest pacer that ever lived." [5]

Dan Patch was shipped home on December 5, 1909. When he arrived at his stable on the Minnesota River, his racing career was over.

# 15

# Railroad Magnate

As Dan Patch's career came to an end, M. W. Savage began to look for new opportunities and pursuits. His businesses were still expanding, and he continued to purchase championship standardbred horses, but his life took an altogether unexpected turn when he decided to run for political office.

The impetus for such a project does not seem to have come from Savage himself. In the spring of 1908, following a month-long negotiation in New York to sell Cresceus to a St. Petersburg horseman named Tellemerzin, Savage returned home to find that a committee had been formed to promote his nomination for governor of the state of Minnesota.

Savage was known in the Minneapolis area to be a life-long Republican and a man unafraid of publicly expressing his opinion on matters of importance to him—witness his moralizing on gambling, his opposition to thoroughbred horse raising, and his lobbying for tax relief on the assessment given his horses. He had achieved a level of renown within the worlds of merchandising and harness racing, and beyond that he was a loyal promoter of the state. In fact, along with Dan Patch, he was one of its principal ambassadors to the nation and as well known as any citizen of Minnesota.

Savage had himself fed that fame by his willingness to offer details of his personal life in the service of his company. The pages of his catalogs continued to tell of the successes of his own career—the fabulous homes, the famed horses, the "world's largest" this and that—and these tales were broadcast across the state and nation.

To add to his appeal, Savage also appears to have been genuinely well-liked by those who knew him and worked for him. He remained accessible to both stable hands and society gents and was eager to rectify any wrongs or mistakes in his business practices that were brought to his attention.

And yet, for all this, he remained an unlikely candidate for political office. Savage was a private man who seldom visited the many Minneapolis-based clubs to which he belonged. He preferred to go to his home directly from his office and if possible to the farm, rather than to spend time hobnobbing with society.

Further, the seeming openness he exhibited in his catalogs and the opinions he expressed in local newspapers were always on his own terms, with no discordant voices to challenge his ideas or cast doubts on his point of view. Savage had been his own boss for many years; it was certainly fair to question whether he was capable of being bossed by two million Minnesotans.

"I will admit, that I was somewhat surprised to find people wearing buttons with my picture on them," a nonetheless intrigued Savage told the *Minneapolis Journal* when he learned of attempts to draft him as a candidate. "What I once thought was a joke, I am now ready to take under consideration with some seriousness. I am not a politician, but realize that it is an age of commercialism, and that Minnesota, if it keeps to the fore, must push out." [1]

Savage obviously found the challenge of the campaign appealing. Perhaps, like so many self-made men in his day (and ours), he had developed such a deep faith in his own ability to make things happen that entering the realm of politics seemed simply like a new enterprise to pursue and conquer. Whatever the case may have been, M. W. Savage entered the rough and tumble world of Minnesota politics on May 8, 1908, when he formally announced his candidacy for governor.

Savage labeled himself "the business men's candidate" and chose as the slogan for his campaign "Savage will help Minnesota grow"—not exactly scintillating stuff, especially for an old ad man. But Will Savage understood that he would not win on the strength of his political acumen. "I am free to admit that I am not a politician and am inexperienced in extended political campaigns," he said in his first campaign speech, "and yet I believe that fair and square business methods will appeal to the people in a state election as much as in general business activities." [2]

The governor's seat was held by a popular Democrat, John Johnson, who would be running for reelection in the fall. Before he could challenge Johnson, however, M. W. Savage had a formidable hurdle to overcome within his own Republican party. To become the GOP candidate for governor, Savage needed first to win his party's nomination, and to do that, he had to secure the support of the Hennepin County Republican party delegation prior to the state party's nominating convention. This was no minor step. Savage was faced with a tough challenge from another Hennepin Country Republican, a Civil War veteran named Captain Samuel P. Snider.

If there were any deep issues dividing Savage and Snider, they weren't immediately evident. Savage declared himself a candidate "absolutely independent of party factions and free from political trickery or special interests." He also said that he was running a campaign "free of combinations," meaning he was not part of any bloc of office-seekers within the Republican Party. "I am not a candidate of any interest or set of interests, nor am I supported by any organized crowd of politicians. If the people are satisfied to trust their affairs to my keeping I shall do everything in my power to serve them and shall appreciate the honor." [3]

But in fact Savage was supported by an organized crowd of politicians of his own; there just weren't as many in his camp as in Snider's. And while his emphasis in campaign bulletins and newspaper articles continued to tout his business acumen, it did not suggest just how his experiences were going to aid the electorate.

The Hennepin County Republican Convention was a raucous gathering held in Minneapolis at the end of June. Neither candidate was in attendance, but both were well-represented by a loud contingent of supporters. The gathering was described by the *Journal* as "the liveliest convention in years," and its chairman was moved to remind delegates at the outset of the evening "that we are Republicans first and fighters afterward." [4]

There were no issues debated at the meeting—or at least none that were reported the next day in The Journal. The main point of the gathering was simply to vote on the two candidates, and the winner would be he who had marshaled his delegates best prior to the get-together. That turned out to be Captain Snider, who beat M. W. Savage by 27 votes, 262 to 235.

At the end of the long evening, Will Savage's political career came to an abrupt end. Samuel Snider's came to an end a few months later, when John Johnson was re-elected governor of the state of Minnesota.

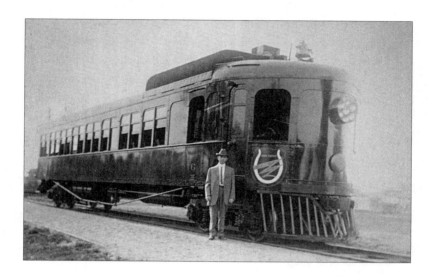

## The Dan Patch Line

Savage spent little time licking his wounds. In fact, he'd already begun his last and, in some regards, his greatest enterprise, the year before his ill-fated foray into politics.

In 1907 a fast-talking Easterner named William P. Mason, who had no money but knew something about railroads, approached Savage with a plan to create a line that would run from downtown Minneapolis to the town of Savage, a distance of twenty miles. There, scads of excursionists would be deposited within walking distance of the great Dan Patch and the beautiful International Stock Food Farm. [5]

It seemed a natural link to Savage, and he not only bit on the idea but almost immediately began to expand on it. In March of that year, M. W. announced to the papers that he was forming a railroad company that would build a line not just to the farm but all the way into northern Iowa. "I am convinced that there is in no richer country in the United States than that which will be tapped by the Dan Patch air line. This country is practically without north and south railroad facilities and the line will be a great boon to the inhabitants," said Savage, who also predicted that the railroad would add $10 million to Minneapolis commerce.

By July of 1907 the Minneapolis, St. Paul, Rochester & Dubuque Traction Company, otherwise known as the Dan Patch Air Line, was incorporated. Expanding further on the original plan, Savage decided that a passenger line was also needed between Minneapolis, the communities of southern Minnesota and northern Iowa, and then all the way east from Dubuque to Chicago. It was going to be a special line, too, thoroughly modern. The railroad was going to run electric cars to insure a clean and comfortable ride.

 These electric locomotives, the forerunners of diesel/electric engines that would power train travel in decades to come, burned gasoline to produce electrical power to propel and control the railroad cars. The General Electric Company, which had pioneered the technology, had begun producing cars in 1908, just as Will Savage was getting involved in the railroad industry. The first two cars purchased by the Dan Patch Line, however, the Irene and the Augerita, came from an inter-urban railroad company in Kansas City.

M. W. Savage was made President and Treasurer of the company, and its officers included T. W. Patterson, owner of a wholesale furrier company in Minneapolis, and an attorney, M. H. Boutelle of Minneapolis. In time, Will Savage's son Erle would come on board as a director, along with a pair of prominent real estate developers, an International Sugar Feed Company executive named W. J. Morris, and a Minneapolis Chamber of Commerce officer.

The company started selling stock at $25 a share, with an emphasis on pitching the idea of the railroad to the farmers and citizens living along the length of the proposed track. That meant M. W. Savage's neighbors in Bloomington, Savage, and the towns south of the farm, including Lakeville, Northfield, and Faribault, would become an intricate part of the enterprise.

The Dan Patch Line made a populist appeal to area residents: There were to be "no big fish to swallow the little ones" in this company;

93 percent of its first stockholders held less than five shares a piece, according to an early prospectus prepared by the company. M. W. Savage, "one of the best known advertising and individual business men in the world" would guarantee a return. "President Savage is a man after the people's own heart," the prospectus proclaimed, "and as President of the Dan Patch Electric Railroad—the People's Railroad—he will prove a safe partner for all those who become stockholders with him."

There were 700,000 people living along the line of the proposed track, which included some of the richest farming territory in the nation. In the Minnesota counties alone, farm values were put at more than 140 million dollars. The region produced five million bushels of barley, 23 million bushels of buckwheat, 9 million bushels of corn, and more than 7 million dozens of eggs.

While an electric railroad might seem unusual, and therefore risky, to a farmer without a lot of investment capital, there were moneymaking electric railroads all across the country, according to the company. A passenger could travel from New York to Chicago entirely on electric trains, it claimed. Four hundred million dollars had been earned by electric train companies in the nation in 1909. Electric trains ran clean, comfortable, and fast, at a rate "as high as one hundred miles per hour with perfect safety."

The Dan Patch Line would connect to the southern end of the Minneapolis streetcar system at Fifty-Fourth Street and Nicollet. Heading from that terminus southward, the line would need to be constructed through Richfield and Bloomington. Then a bridge needed to be built over the Minnesota River to the International Stock Food Farm. From there, the line would continue south through farmland to Northfield and Faribault.

Construction to the town of Savage began as Will Savage was heading his gubernatorial race in 1908. Track was laid from Bloomington down into the Minnesota River valley and rights of way were purchased for the track to continue on to Northfield, a run of thirty-five miles from Minneapolis. An immediate concern arose, however. The Dan Patch was initially intended to be a passenger line, but beyond Savage's

International Stock Food Farm, which was itself in the countryside, all the way to Northfield, there were no communities, and no points of destination. In time, this corridor would contain Interstate 35 and be home to some of the densest exurban sprawl in the Twin Cities metropolitan area, but in Dan Patch's day there were not enough bodies in the region to cart to and from the cities to help finance the continued construction of the line.

To help alleviate the problem, M. W. Savage decided to generate his own traffic southward. The company purchased 237 acres of rolling

MINNESOTA'S BEAUTY PARK

ANTLERS PARK

LAKE MARION. ON THE
DAN PATCH ELECTRIC LINE

countryside in Lakeville on either side of the road to Northfield. There Savage constructed one of the region's first amusement centers, Antler's Park. A Ferris wheel, merry-go-round, and pavilion converted from an old barn were constructed as diversions. In time would come an aerial swing and a midget railway. There was a baseball diamond with a grandstand, cottages available for weekly or monthly stays, a lake at the heart of the playground, which became Lake Marion (after the President of the Dan Patch Line), and boat landings, beaches, and "a bather's chute" to give access to the water. A clubhouse and restaurant were to come.

With this new addition to the Minnesota recreational scene in place, construction on the line quickly progressed southward through Bloomington over the Minnesota River and past Dan Patch and his fellow harness racing stars grazing and training at the International Stock Food Farm.

On July 4, 1910 the railroad arrived at the newly created Antler's Park, which quickly became a popular destination for excursionists from the Twin Cities. In particular, college groups found the amusement park a must-do trip. They would gather at the pavilion where sundaes and sodas were sold, but no liquor. The pavilion had a dance floor made of fine wood, with chandeliers hanging from the ceiling and murals all along the walls. A vine-covered walk passed along the open side of the dance floor. Well-known orchestras appeared there often, and dances were ten cents for a set of three.

Electrical power at the park was generated by an off-duty engine from the Dan Patch Line, pulled to a siding on the grounds.

Meanwhile, the Dan Patch Line hummed onward toward Northfield, which it reached on December 1, 1910, just five months after the line had opened to Antler's Park. The first car to pull into the station, the Irene, carried Savage and the board of directors of the Minneapolis, St. Paul, Rochester and Dubuque Electric Traction Company.

The *Northfield News* was impressed: "The news that the first car over the Dan Patch line had arrived in the city spread quickly, and the Irene was soon surrounded by an interested and curious crowd. An inspection of the car brought a pleasant surprise to everyone. Not even the finest observation cars on the coast trains are better or more comfortably equipped than the Irene. Every convenience is provided, with a few additional ones peculiar only to electric transportation added. A more pleasant means of conveyance could not be imagined. Among those who visited the car were some of the doubting Thomases, who at last, with the reality before their eyes, admitted that the 'thing was really a go.'"

The man who was most responsible for making this happen basked in the triumph. "The completion of this electric line to Northfield should prove the opening of a new and auspicious era in the history of the city," Savage remarked to a *Northfield New* reporter. There was more work to do, however: "It but remains for the citizens to act while the time is opportune and advertise Northfield's advantages as they have never been advertised before. Publicity, backed by faith in the facts presented, is all that Northfield needs in order to attract a large number of very desirable residents." [7]

## Dan in Retirement

Although the champion's racing days were over, a sighting of Dan Patch remained a highlight of any trip along the Dan Patch Line. The fabulous International Stock Food Farm, which Savage had renamed the International 1:55 Horse Breeding Farm in 1907, continued to attract tourists and horse fans, and Dan remained a living icon of harness racing. His place in the hearts of harness racing fans across the country remained secure even if he was no longer a part of the turf world. To prove the point a 1911 poll taken by the *Horse Review* asked its readers to judge the 10 greatest pacers of all time. Out of 3,524 votes cast, Dan Patch collected 2,901. The nearest horse to him was his father, Joe Patchen, who received a mere 210 votes.[8]

The year before the poll, in 1910, Dan had traveled with the impressive Savage racing team of Minor Heir, Hedgewood Boy, Lady Maud C, and George Gano on a national tour of the harness racing circuit. Dan, decked out in gold-mounted harness and with a decorated sulky, had only been exhibited, "not asked to lower any world records," according to the *Minneapolis Journal*; however, he had occasionally been allowed to "step through the stretch … at his old-time speed."

In September 1911 he made his final trip to the Minnesota State Fair, again in the company of the new Savage racing team. Here, at the scene of some his greatest triumphs, Dan held public receptions in a large tent set up expressly for the purpose while his stable mates took center stage at the track. Dan was said to be interested in the doings of Minor Heir, George Gano, Hedgewood Boy, and Lady Maud C, but the claim of one Minneapolis reporter that "those who know the great horse best believe he knows what these other great pacers are striving for and is interested in the results" seems a little farfetched.

The International Stock Food Farm also entered a long string of Dan's offspring in various harness racing divisions at the state fair competition. By that time there were scores of Patch children racing for Savage and other breeders. Those at the fair included Mary E. Patch, Rena Patch, Queen Patch, Princess Patch, Flossie Patch, Marion Patch, and Madge Patch.

Dan's old driver, Hersey, had moved on to take the reins of Minor Heir, a post which he would hold for several more years before leaving Savage's employ in 1913 to become a driver and trainer for an Indianapolis stock farm.[9]

Back at the 1:55 Farm under the continuing care of longtime handler Charley Plummer, Dan Patch led a pretty good life. In his *Autobiography*, M. E. Harrison had Dan describe his own retirement: "My day begins at five o'clock in the morning with a breakfast of four quarts of well-screened oats. My caretaker always keeps a bucket of fresh water in my stall so that I can drink when and as much as I like."

Dan was stabled in a comfortable "apartment" twenty feet square with hot water, electricity, and plenty of ventilation. The windows were fitted with shades to keep his stable cool in the summer "and dark for my noon rests."

There was always a plentiful supply of fresh straw on hand, which was banked several feet high against each wall to prevent injuries to Dan when he was rolling in the stall. A cord was strung, about four feet from the floor, clear around the stall and on it were hung Dan's special monogrammed, woolen blankets, "forming a decoration as well as a protection." [10]

After Dan's morning meal, he was taken on a jog of five or six miles followed by a cooling out period, and then returned to the stall, where woolen bandages were put on his legs. Then came lunch and an afternoon nap.

"At 4:30 the stall is put in order and I am again given a bunch of timothy hay and water. At five o'clock I get four quarts of cooked oats and bran. After this meal the feed-box is removed and I am carefully prepared for the night."

As for his general surroundings, Dan was comfortable, according to M. E. Harrison: "The stables are as large and complete as any in the world. The five great wings radiating from the immense rotunda together with a long barn immediately in the rear provide stall accommodations for fully two hundred and twenty-five horses. The entire plant is lighted acetylene gas, piped with water and hot water heated. Everything is peaceful and well ordered and it is an ideal place for a retired champion to spend his latter days."

By all accounts, M. W. Savage maintained a deep affinity for Dan throughout his retirement. Even Ken McCarr, who had a far less sentimental view of M. W. Savage than M. E. Harrison, agreed that horse and owner had an uncommon bond. "As a horse lover, [Savage's] enthusiasm and interest centered on Dan Patch," he wrote in a 1970s recollection of the pair. "It is doubtful that any owner of a great horse more deeply loved or more intensely appreciated the animal than Savage did where Dan Patch was concerned. It could almost be said that Dan was a part of his owner's religion for his attachment to the great pacer bordered on idolatry." [11]

Fred Sasse, author of *The Great Dan Patch*, a book written in the 1950s, met both horse and owner at a first visit to The International 1:55 Stock Farm back in 1913. Sasse came to the grounds as a young artist, hoping to land a job with the International Stock Food Company catalogs. He was a small-town Minnesota boy who had just arrived in the Twin Cities looking for work. He liked to draw horses and had sketched Dan Patch from photographs many times before; now he had a chance to visit the farm and actually see the great horse in the flesh.

"Thousands had already made and were still making pilgrimages to this sacred Mecca of horsedom," Sasse wrote of that first visit, "even though Dan had been retired to the stud. Men, women, and children were daily visitors at this huge plant. That I was welcome was plainly evident."

According to Sasse's account, he was escorted around the farm by none other than Harry Hersey, who introduced him to a mild-mannered man wearing a dark business suit and derby hat. This turned out to be M. W. Savage, who joined the tour and lead them all down one of the wings of the giant stable, passing a dozen white-painted box stalls lining either side of the barn. "Grooms bustled about their morning chores. Savage saluted [them], calling each by name."

Finally, they came to Dan Patch's stall. Savage opened the lower door to the space and invited Sasse inside. "There I saw what millions of people have longed to see; what I had wanted to see for years—Dan Patch in the flesh." Savage walked through the deep straw to the stallion and patted his beautiful neck. The horse laid his head on his master's shoulder. Dan's owner then pulled the woolen, checkered blanket over the sleek rump to display the shiny brown coat which shone like a polished jewel.

"How are you, Dan old boy?" Savage caressed him. "How's my big boy this morning?"

It could hardly have been a more exciting visit for a young lover of horses. And whether or not each detail was true doesn't seem quite the point of Sasse's story. What he was trying to convey was the experience of the thousands of Dan's fans who made the same pilgrimage to the 1:55 Farm in those years of the champion's retirement. For all those farm kids who'd grown up eating meals beneath the image of Dan Patch in the family kitchen, this was a special moment. Savage, no doubt, understood that feeling.

"I wish everyone felt as though they had a share of this animal." Sasse quotes him as saying. "I feel a little greedy owning him all myself when he has so many friends."[12]

No records survive of the number of visitors who came to see Dan Patch at the International 1:55 Stock Farm. Nor are there accurate totals of how many race fans might have seen the great pacer in his prime or have held the image of Dan Patch in the mind the way Sasse did, courtesy of M. W. Savage's advertising.

What seems clear is that there were millions who did feel they owned a share of Dan Patch.

# 16

# Trains, Horses, and Automobiles

Well before the United States finally entered World War I in 1917, U.S. traders were shipping tens of thousands of horses every month to serve in the cavalry and artillery units of the allied armies in Europe. Horse buyers for the British, French, Italian, and Greek armies scoured the markets in Chicago, St. Louis, Kansas City, and other smaller cities throughout the Midwest, and turned their attention even further westward as the war progressed. The hapless horses, upon their arrival in Europe, were trained to stay as calm as possible in the face of explosions from pistols, rifles, cannon, and bombs. At that point they were considered ready for duty on the front lines. Few of them survived the ordeal. [1]

Although the horses often met with a gruesome fate, the horse-traders themselves made profits like they hadn't in years. The market for horses had been on the wane in the U.S. for quite some time due to the growing popularity of automobiles, farm tractors, and trucks. In 1915 there were more than thirty-four thousand tractors in use on American farms, and just one of these vehicles could plow, disk, and seed twenty-five acres of farmland a day—work that took one man and a team of horses two weeks to accomplish. In the massive national effort to produce guns and butter for the war, it was almost unpatriotic not to see the merits of tractor use.

There were other utilitarian arguments against the value of horses in these war-strapped times. It was estimated that $130,000,000 worth of leather was used each year to make harnesses. "Charge it to the horse if you have to pay more than ever for your shoes," wrote a reporter in *McClure's*. New York spent $50,000,000 cleaning its streets every year; if horses were banned from the city, it was thought that the cost would drop to $10,000,000. It was also said that there was enough iron used in making horseshoes in the U.S. to fashion 40,000 tractors or 60,000 trucks.

The U.S. Bureau of Animal Industry estimated that there were about 24,000,000 horses in the United States at the start of the war. In the six months prior to the war, the value of those animals had fallen 33 percent below the norm. A year into the war, horses were valued at 25 per cent above the norm. And that shift wasn't simply because supply was low; in fact, for all the animals heading to Europe, there remained plenty to be had in the United States.

"The war business in horses is a good thing for this country any way you look at it," said *Collier's* magazine in a brutal assessment published in September 1915. "It will not seriously deplete the country's stock of horses. And it is making money for the farmer, for the railroads, for the ship owners, for the contractors, for the men who are supplying the feed, shoes, halters, disinfectants, medicines, and for numberless others, all along the line.

"The only fellow who is not benefiting is—the horse. And if he must go to feed the cannons, well, there are better than he doing the same. And for this human cannon food there is no credit balance to any one."

## The Dan Patch Line

M. W. Savage was not in the business of selling cannon fodder to the armies of Europe, but his Dan Patch Line, like so many other advances in transportation over the previous twenty years, was helping to speed the end of the horse-and-carriage era. While it's doubtful the trainloads of college-age excursionists spying Dan Patch in retirement at the International 1:55 were yet thinking of him as a quaint icon from a bygone era, the fact of the matter was that most were speeding by him to enjoy the modern amusements at Antler's Park, and Dan was fast becoming yesterday's news.

The parking lot at Antler's Park

Antler's Park remained a Twin Cities hotspot. Within a year of its opening, the number of visitors had increased to such an extent that the Dan Patch Line began buying brand-new General Electric cars—eventually thirteen were purchased—to help haul the extra traffic.

But despite the crowds heading to the park, not all was well with the railroad. Savage was having trouble buying the rights-of-way through the city of Faribault, eighteen miles to the south of Northfield and the next major stop on the route to Iowa. The Minneapolis, St. Paul, Rochester & Dubuque Electric Traction

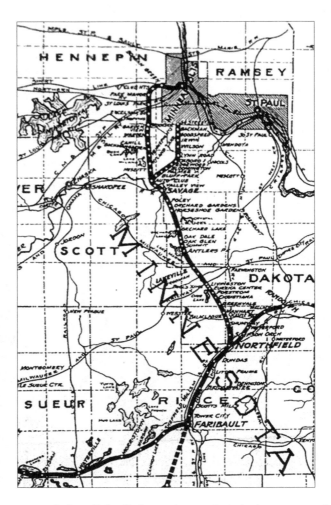

Company needed to link all the major stations in its name to be the sort of profitable regional passenger carrier that Savage had envisioned. To come to a halt in Faribault, less than sixty miles from its start in Minneapolis, would be a crippling blow to the company.

To boost the traffic on his existing line and help finance the continued construction of the railroad, the Dan Patch Line began hauling freight. It also began construction on a fifteen-mile track extension from the Auto Club near Savage's home in Bloomington through the then sparsely populated western suburbs of Minneapolis, Edina, and St. Louis

Park. This loop would ultimately lead to a junction that would take the Dan Patch right to downtown Minneapolis and its own station located at North Seventh Street and Third Avenue North. It was a line that at a later date would describe one of the principal highway loops of the metropolitan region, just as the rest of the Dan Patch line to Northfield would one day describe the major interstate highway to Iowa.

But Savage's railroad would get no points for prescience in regard to future metropolitan growth. It was being built before the region was densely populated. For the time being the company needed money to pay for the extra line, the new station, and the purchase of more engines for its expanding freight and passenger usage—as well as the continued effort to buy right-of-way into Faribault and beyond. Once again, the Dan Patch Line needed to go to its investors with an offer of more shares in the railroad.

It was starting to be a tough sale for Will Savage. His stockholders had yet to receive dividends on their initial holdings, and there were already whisperings among them about the fashion in which the company was being run. It was said that certain personal and corporate extravagances were being charged to the business to no great benefit to its investors. There were rumors that large chunks of the advertising budget for the railroad were in fact hyping the 1:55 stock farm and that postage fees for farm mailings were being charged to the Dan Patch Line.

"The Marion," the jewel of the railroad's passenger cars, was fitted out in lush style, with stained glass windows, leather club chairs, and an interior decorated by fine draperies and beautiful rare woods. The company itself advertised the vehicle as the "Most Beautiful and Expensive General Service Car in the World," but the gossip was that it saw less general than personal use. The claim was that it had essentially become the car of its namesake, the president of the company, and other company officers. [2]

The downtown Minneapolis offices of the electric railroad company occupied a full floor of the Jewelry Exchange Building at Seventh Street and First Avenue, and according to a newspaper reporter of the day—obviously suggesting the exclusivity of the procedure—to get an appointment, "one stepped into an outer lobby and sent his card in through suites of offices to ... the particular one that he desired to have speech with." [3]

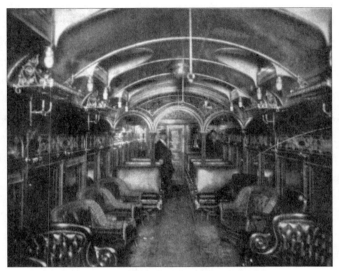

The lavish interior of the "Marion" rail car

The Dan Patch railroad had been born as a high-class passenger line, however, and M. W. Savage wasn't about to skimp on amenities now. Impressing his clients with style and his own personal successes had always been a sales strategy for Savage. That's why his advertising featured The World's Greatest Pacer. That's why it was littered with photos of his beautiful homes in Bloomington, Minneapolis, and Wayzata. That's why he loved to tell his rag-to-riches story in his catalog pages and proudly proclaim his ownership of "The Largest Food Company in the World" with its "largest single office space."

Of course, Savage had always been in the business of selling products to his customers; now he was asking them to partner with him on the Dan Patch Line, which was a different equation.

"It is absolutely necessary for the Dan Patch Electric Line to have the additional mileage to and the large Business from the Splendid

Cities of Faribault and Owatonna and also to complete the work into our New, Down Town Minneapolis Terminal—to be on a dividend paying basis," he wrote to a stockholder in February 1913. "You want Quick Dividends on the stock you have already purchased—so do eight thousand other stockholders. I am very anxious that the Dan Patch Electric Line shall become a regular dividend payer at the earliest possible date. It will be one of the happiest moments of my business life when I can sign a dividend check for your stock. You won't feel half as good about it as I will because the dividend checks will be absolute proof that big enterprise can be handled by the people." [4]

This populist appeal to investors no doubt had a different ring to their ears now, several years into the project, especially given all those whispers about the special privileges being granted M. W. Savage and the company's top management.

In fact there were more serious matters at hand for Savage and company than just rumors of excess. Simply put, the railroad was costing too much. The rights of way were too expensive and so was the equipment. It had purchased the most modern gas/electric cars being made, bought 50 percent of a station in downtown Minneapolis, and laid nearly 60 miles of track in all, and it still hadn't gotten out of Northfield. All of that line had been laid at a cost of $210,000 a mile, as compared to the average steam railroad line in America, which was constructed for around $65,000 a mile. [5]

Though it began leasing track rights to Faribault and Owatonna from the Chicago Great Western Railway (an arrangement that would last only one year), the fact of the matter was that any additional revenue that it accrued through this arrangement was too little and too late and had to be shared with the Great Western. The Dan Patch Line was not going to succeed on day-trippers waving at Dan Patch on their way to Antler's Park.

M. W. Savage's appeals to the stockholders were sounding more and more strained as he continued to search for money to finish the line into downtown Minneapolis as well as southward through

Faribault: "Something must be done at once," is how Savage opened a January 1914 letter to stockholders. "This is the most important letter I have ever written to you. Are you interested in having the Dan Patch Electric Line finish the necessary mileage to make it a quick dividend payer?"

An overpass on the Dan Patch line

Savage, always unafraid of making a personal appeal, did so once again: "I am trying to constantly work for your best interest—as well as for the best interests of all stockholders—in getting the Dan Patch Electric Line on an early dividend paying basis but to do this—certain things must be done, as I have outlined in a previous letter."

But it was all starting to sound like a pretty desperate pitch: "Any railroad expert in the world will tell you that our Earnings and Profits will Tremendously Increase—just as soon as our line is completed to Owatonna and connection is made with our new, private right of way, to the Business Center of Minneapolis, one of the Big, Fast Growing Cities of the world." [6]

By the end of May 1915 the Dan Patch railroad had completed fourteen miles of line from the Auto Club in Bloomington to the junction leading into Minneapolis, but it would take another year for the depot at Seventh Avenue and Third Street to be finished. In the mean time the struggles with rights-of-way and the community of Faribault continued.

In a bid to help push his train line further south, M. W. Savage secured a loan from an organization called the Faribault Commercial Club. In exchange, the railroad promised to locate company shops—sheds for the maintenance of Dan Patch railway cars—in Faribault. But a year after this agreement had been made, the shops were still not in the town, and what was worse from the Commercial Club point-of-view, the Dan Patch Line was now in obvious financial difficulty. At the start of the year 1916 it had just suspended all service to Faribault by ending its leasing agreement with the Chicago Great Western line.

In a June letter to M. W. Savage, the Chairman of the Commercial Club, W. S. Shaft, was politely blunt about the problem. Money had been lent and now money was owed, but there were still no car shops in Faribault: "I respectfully urge that you give me your immediate service as to what you intend to do with reference to the notes placed with our citizens." [7]

Shaft and the Commercial Club would be disappointed in the answer they received on a number of counts. First of all, the reply was from counsel for the railroad company, M. H. Boutelle, and not M. W. Savage, who in the public's estimation as well as in the estimation of the Commercial Club of Faribault, was the heart and soul of the company.

Secondly, with regard to the shops, the news was not good. "While the company's experiences under its Great Western leases had not ... been satisfactory," Boutelle explained, "the opinion of the new management was that with the opening of the new downtown terminal in Minneapolis, the results would be reflected all along the line. Unfortunately," Boutelle continued, "this expectation was not realized, and to put the matter in perfectly plain parlance, the experience with Great Western property pretty nearly broke the back of the Dan Patch enterprise."

Other news from the attorney was equally discouraging. The reason he was responding rather than Savage himself was that the president of the railroad was in the hospital, and not well. The prospects of getting any satisfaction from the Dan Patch Line without dealing directly with Savage were slim.

"At this writing," Boutelle informed the Faribault Commercial Club, "Mr. Savage is confined to the hospital, having recently undergone a comparatively unpleasant but, fortunately, not a critical operation. His convalescence is now progressing satisfactorily and he will doubtless be able to resume his active work within the next few weeks."

Boutelle tried to offer some solace: "I am not personally in position to definitely speak for Mr. Savage," he wrote, but, "I know it was his belief, as it was that of the rest of us, that Faribault would be selected as the location of the shops."

It's doubtful the Commercial Club of Faribault was assuaged by this opinion, nor would it find any more satisfaction in the news that was soon to come.

The unpleasant, but not critical, operation that M. W. Savage had recently undergone was surgery for acute hemorrhoids. No doubt the stress of his work was unhelpful to his condition, but as Boutelle suggested, there was nothing extraordinarily perilous about his circumstances. Unfortunately, worse was to come.

PHOTOGRAPH OF DAN PATCH 1:55¼ AT FASTEST SPEED, WITH EVERY FOOT OFF THE GROUND.

# 17

# Last Laps

ill Savage turned fifty-seven years old that year. As far as is known, his health had been good in the years leading up to his hospitalization in July 1916, but it's likely that he felt a deep distress over the circumstances of the railroad as he recovered from his surgery. On the other hand, his Savage Factories, including the Stock Food Company and his merchandising business, continued to do good business and were worth in excess of fifteen million dollars (about a quarter of a billion dollars in current exchange). His livestock business was doing fairly well, as were his Sugar Feed Companies in Minneapolis and Memphis. Yet this was a man unaccustomed to failing, and the circumstances surrounding the Dan Patch Line could be described in no other way. There is no record of his thoughts or concerns as he lay in his hospital bed, contemplating the impending bankruptcy of the Dan Patch Railroad Company, but it's easy to imagine his anguish. After all, 8,500 bondholders of the Dan Patch Line—many of them the farmers and townspeople of southern Minnesota, fans of Dan Patch, and faithful customers of the International Stock Food Company—were holding shares of essentially valueless stock which they had bought on his word, through his salesmanship, through his assurance that he was one of them, a man of the people, guaranteeing that this railroad was bound to be a success.

Never had M. W. Savage had a failing like this one.

Out at the farm, some twenty miles from where Will Savage lay, Dan Patch was not doing so well, either. On the same Friday that his owner went into the hospital, Patch developed a slight sickness that seemed to disappear on Sunday, only to return again the next evening.

A groomsman named Mike Egan and a trainer at the farm, Murray Anderson, were attending to Dan. A Minneapolis veterinarian was called as well, but on Tuesday morning, July 11, 1916, the horse took a sudden turn for the worse and collapsed in his stall.

With a sickening sense, his trainers quickly realized that they were caring for a mortally ill animal. According to the *St. Paul Pioneer Press,* "Until a few seconds before he breathed his last, he was standing in his stall with his head erect. As he sank to the ground the wonderful feet which earned fame and fortune for his owner began to move like piston rods, as though he was stepping over a course with a large purse awaiting his owner at the end of the race. This continued for several seconds and then, with a gasp, the noble animal was dead." [1]

Members of the Savage family had been contacted as Dan collapsed, but his condition deteriorated so rapidly that no one from the family was available to witness his demise. The veterinarian, Dr. Charles Cotton, declared the cause of death to be an "athletic heart," meaning that Dan's abnormally large heart muscle prompted a fatal attack.

According to Sasse, Dan Patch's heart weighed nine pounds and two ounces at the time of his death as compared to a "normal weight" for a horse of his size of five pounds. He does not tell us who weighed the horse's heart, nor does he suggest, beyond this reference to the size of the heart, that any sort of autopsy was done.

In any event, Dan was twenty years old at the time of his death. He had worked extremely hard for most of those years, racing for ten seasons and traveling distances that few other animals had measured. His body was no doubt tired, and his time had come.

By all accounts, Dan was good-natured until the very end. He loved crowds and the hubbub that surrounded his life. That he was cherished by those closest to him is without doubt. Those who saw him race held the image in their minds for years afterward—a testament to his greatness as an athlete. He was the supreme harness racing horse of his day in an era when that made him an icon of speed, grace, and beauty for millions of people across the nation. But he was also a horse, and his racing days had been over for years. In Europe the Battle of the Somme was raging; off the coast of New Jersey, a series of shark attacks were terrorizing the eastern seaboard. Notice of his death was published over much of the country from the *New York Times* to the *Chicago Tribune*. But except in the local news, his death would not claim the column inches that his racing successes had at the height of his career.

Whatever Dan Patch might have been thinking in the hours and days leading up to his passing, those musings would probably not resemble human sentimentality. Still it's hard to resist hoping that Dan Patch left this earth with the knowledge that he was loved, that he had moved faster than any horse who had ever raced against him, and that he was a magnificent creature.

The only question now was, who would tell Mr. Savage that he was gone?

The Savage family was reluctant to break the news to M. W. Savage in his already debilitated state, fearing that it would distress him too much. But after some hemming and hawing, it was finally agreed that he had to be told, and it fell to Murray Anderson, the trainer, to make the call.

Dan Patch had died at 10 a.m. on Tuesday, July 11. Anderson phoned Mr. Savage with the news that day. All who saw Savage that evening and the next day agree that the death of Dan Patch was a shock to his system. But he was well enough to take calls of condolences from friends and fans of Dan Patch. He also apparently talked with Anderson

Marietta Savage

about plans that he had devised a year earlier for Dan's burial. He wanted the horse stuffed and mounted and then buried on the farm "beneath a certain oak tree" where other Savage horses, including Buttonwood, Roy Wilkes, and Online had been buried.

Savage's wife, Marietta, along with hospital staff, felt that her husband was doing much better by the time she left his side at five o'clock on Wednesday afternoon, July 12. She headed back toward the family home in Bloomington for the evening, but at some point in that half-hour ride, something went terribly wrong. Word came to her the moment she arrived in Bloomington that her husband was now deathly ill and that she should speed back to the hospital.

According to newspaper accounts in both the *St. Paul Pioneer Press* and the *Minneapolis Tribune*, Marietta Savage didn't even get out of the car but immediately turned around and headed back into the city. She arrived back at the hospital too late. At 6 p.m. Marion Willis Savage was dead, hardly more than a day after his beloved horse, Dan Patch, had

# M. W. SAVAGE, RAIL BUILDER, HORSEMAN, MANUFACTURER, DIES

M. W. Savage holding Dan Patch. This picture, taken eight years ago, was Mr. Savage's favorite photograph.

**End Follows Death of Beloved Horse, Dan Patch, by Only 32 Hours—Savage Widely Known as Electric Railroad Builder.**

M. W. Savage, who for 30 years was a constructive force in the commercial life of Minneapolis, and whose name, carried abroad by his interest in stock breeding, probably was more widely known

side, and the utilization of the mammoth structure for the enlarged factory, was a deal of such interest in real estate circles and industrially that it at once gave Mr. Savage marked business prominence in Minneapolis.

Thereafter he built the International Sugar Feed plant in southeast Minneapolis and another at Memphis, Tenn., extending his business interests also to Toronto, Ont., and other cities. His latest commercial extension was of the M. W. Savage factories, incorporated, the business of which, carried on for a short time in the exposition buildi-

departed this world. A pulmonary embolism was listed as the cause of death, with the acute hemorrhoids mentioned as a contributing factor. M. W. Savage had died quickly.

"Partners in business, they were now partners in death," Fred Sasse wrote.

"Mr. Savage's life was peculiarly linked with that of his great horse," wrote the *Minneapolis Tribune*, "so much so that his friends last night spoke of the possible effect Dan Patch's death may have had in hastening the death of his owner. The horse brought the man wealth and fame and it is universally known that Mr. Savage's affection for Dan Patch was as great as man ever bore animal." [2]

The *Chicago Tribune* was more succinct: "The death of Mr. Savage so suddenly after that of Dan Patch seems like a queer turn of fate."

On Saturday, July 15, the two of them were buried at the same hour in separate parts of the cities. Savage was laid to rest in Lakewood Cemetery near the lakes of Minneapolis, among the Pillsburys, the Washburns, the Kelloggs, and other civic leaders and social luminaries. Dan Patch was buried beneath an oak tree that Savage had designated at the International 1:55 Farm in the Minnesota River Valley.

The family squelched plans to have Dan Patch stuffed—rumor had it that it was Marietta who thought the idea excessive—and it fell to Anderson and Mike Egan, the pair of handlers who'd been with Patch at the end, to bury him. They did so without ceremony and without marking the spot.

As word of Dan Patch's death spread, Anderson received letters from a number of veterinarian colleges, offering large sums for the horse's body, but Savage's family knew this would never have met with his approval.

No one would ever see the body of Dan Patch again. And as it turned out, no one but the two undertakers would ever know just where the great horse was buried. There is no longer a giant oak tree on the property, and Anderson and Egan never spread the word about where it might have been. To this day the mystery of Dan's whereabouts remains a source of speculation in the town of Savage and among the remaining devotees of the Dan Patch saga.

## End of the Line

The obituaries for M. W. Savage told of his origins as a farmboy in Iowa, the beginnings of his career in Minneapolis, the great successes of his International Stock Food Company, his merchandising enterprise, and his stock farm, and, of course, his purchase of Dan Patch and the fabulous racing career that ensued. M. W. Savage had been a Minnesotan for almost thirty years, and for nearly half of that time, he had been one of the region's most renowned citizens and a leading ambassador of the state to the country at large. There was little point in dwelling on his troubled railroad enterprise. Better to remember the brilliant entrepreneur, the innovative marketer, the man who in his own words "was born with a great desire to raise high-class harness horse" and wound up doing just that.

Only the *Minneapolis Journal* mentioned the railroad, and they were delicate. "Against all the difficulties that a pioneer in a new field must encounter, [Savage] organized the Minneapolis, St. Paul, Rochester & Dubuque Electric Traction Company, known as The Dan Patch Line," the paper said. "This company built southward from the city, opening up a rich territory … the value of this work to the city was great."

Savage was survived by his wife, Marietta, sons Erle and Harold, and his sister, Mrs. E. H. Forster. The precise size of his estate was not known, but it was thought to be in the neighborhood of $15 million, which was the approximate value of his merchandising and stock food business.

The Dan Patch Line went into receivership the week after Will Savage's death. According to newspaper accounts, the company had issued nearly $5 million in common stock and an additional $3.36 million in preferred bonds. These, along with additional debts, brought the company's total of unpaid obligations to almost $11 million.[3]

The receivers tried to recoup some of these losses for the stockholders during the following two years by selling a substantial amount of the passenger equipment, as well as Antler's Park, which went for $16,000. The Minneapolis, St. Paul, Rochester & Dubuque Electric Traction Co. itself was purchased at a foreclosure auction in August 1918 by a newly incorporated company called The Minneapolis, Northfield & Southern Railway, which immediately scrapped Savage's ambitious plans for development but continued to operate fifty-two miles of track with three gas-electric passenger cars, four passenger trailers, one steam locomotive, and 60 freight cars. With judicious management, the company continued to provide service to Northfield, and eventually beyond, into the 1940s.[4]

Savage's stock farm had a quicker demise. Son Erle Savage had little interest in breeding champion harness horses, and Harold, though he had a love for horses and ability with them (he would become one of Minnesota's best amateur harness drivers in years to come), was too young to oversee the farm. Murray Anderson stepped in, therefore, to become manager of the operation.

Without Dan Patch, however, the farm lost its luster. It also suffered in the eyes of the horse community by its location. Despite M. W. Savage's oft-stated intention of making Minnesota a breeding capital for standardbred horses, the distance for hauling the best mares of harness racing from farms in Illinois, Indiana, and Kentucky had proven too daunting for most horse-breeders. In the years preceding Dan's death the feeling had already become widespread within the racing community that he was a disappointing sire. He was disappointing, went the conventional wisdom, primarily because he'd been paired with so few quality mares. And these pairings were so few because the farm was in Minnesota.

# Epilogue

In 1919 the hundred or so standardbred horses remaining at the 1:55 were auctioned off to settle the estate of M. W. Savage. The land and the fabulous stables were sold to a local breeder of prize-winning Holstein cattle. The stables didn't last long under new ownership. A devastating fire in 1922 destroyed the main barn and most of what remained of the Taj. By that time a devastating wind had already wrecked the one-of-kind indoor training track.

For a time in the late 1920s, the outdoor track was used as a venue for dog racing, but local interest in that sport quickly died, and the last vestiges of Savage's International 1:55 Farm were gone by World War II. The riverfront property was used as an industrial site to build landing craft for U. S. invasion forces during the war. Today, the Cargill Company owns the land, and with the exception of a few prominent No Trespassing signs, and thickets of brush and small trees, the once-bustling stretch of river bottom land is rough and empty.

The Savage mansion across the river in Bloomington is gone, too. In its place is a Masonic Home built in the early 1950s on the same landscape from which Will Savage once spied his horses across the river.

Four horseshoes worn by Dan Patch himself are embedded beneath the four cornerstones of the structure.

The Savage merchandising companies continued to operate into the 1930s, producing catalogs as late as 1935. The International Sugar Feed Companies in Minneapolis and Memphis lasted longer, into the 1960s in the first instance and into the 1940s in the second. But there are no Savage businesses in operation today.

One by one the visible remains of that glorious partnership between man and horse disappeared from view, until finally only one thing remained: Dan Patch's remarkable racing records. His Lexington record of 1:55 ¼ in the mile stood unchallenged until 1938, when Billy Direct lowered the time to 1:55—matching Dan's celebrated (by not officially sanctioned) Minnesota State Fair time set thirty-two years earlier. Sixty years after Dan set his mark the time had only been lowered by one and two-fifths of a second.

At mid-century, spurred by the upheavals of war and a yearning for simpler times, there was a small Dan Patch revival that centered around the release of a movie, *The Great Dan Patch*. The film told a nostagalia-laced version of Dan's story with only a remote connection to actual events in his life. The *Saturday Evening Post* did a long piece on Dan Patch at about the same time that was subsequently excerpted in *Reader's Digest*. Fred Sasse's book on Dan Patch was first published in the mid-1950s. Since that time, Dan Patch has been remembered periodically by national sports columnists like Red Smith and Frank Deford, by the writers at *Hoofbeats* magazine, and by writers in regional publications in Minnesota and Indiana. There is a street on the Minnesota State Fairgrounds named Dan Patch Avenue. But most importantly, his legend and name have been promoted and carried forward by collectors of the massive amounts of Dan Patch paraphernalia produced by the marketing efforts of Will Savage.

Though not as popular as it was in Dan Patch's day, harness racing has never ceased to attract sports enthusiasts to the Grand Circuit. Colt racing was introduced and grew rapidly in popularity, and racing contests were shortened from best-of-five heats to best-of-three in efforts to attract new fans. Dash races were also introduced at many tracks, which made it possible for the first time to hold races at night.

In 1924 the Hambletonian Society was established to conduct the Hambletonian Stake, which quickly became the most prestigious event in harness racing's Triple Crown. The society now manages more than a hundred races at tracks throughout the East and Midwest and awards millions of dollars in prize money annually. The United States Trotting Association was created in 1939 for the purpose of establishing a more solid foundation of rules for the sport. It continues to license officials and participants, and register horses for racing and breeding purposes.

Where does the memory of Dan Patch himself figure in all of this? Right at the center, it would appear. Every year the Harness Writer's Association gives out a series of awards for various achievements similar to the movie industry's Oscars, with nominees being named in December and the winners announced at a gala the following spring. The writer's association chose to name their awards after the most beloved pacer of all time—Dan Patch.

Meanwhile, the name Savage continues to grace the town that blossomed around the International 1:55 Stock Farm, and the community has grown rapidly in the last twenty years as the metropolitan area of the Twin Cities has expanded east and west along the same Interstate 35 corridor that M. W. Savage envisioned as a route for his Dan Patch Line.

A local group of involved citizens, the Dan Patch Society, meets on a regular basis in Savage to help promote the city, honor its history, and keep alive the legacy of its most famous former resident. They publish a regular newsletter which details their efforts, and they sponsor an annual Dan Patch Days. A similar festival is held annually in Dan's hometown of Oxford, Indiana, to keep the flame of appreciation for Dan burning.

Nowadays there are plenty of other thrills-and-spills events to vie for the attention of the sports enthusiasts, and harness racing will never again draw the attention it did at the turn of the twentieth century, when horses with buggies still dominated the roads and automobiles were few and far between. Yet against long odds, the name Dan Patch lives on. In part, we can thank M. W. Savage for the lasting legacy—his genius for promotion has proved enduring; and linking his business to the racing achievements and the personal charm of Dan Patch was the best move of a very successful business career.

But Dan was always the true star of the show. He was a magnificent animal with a winning personality and unbeatable speed. Those who watched the great pacer smash his own racing records time after time were awed and inspired by his gifts, and cherished him in a way that few other athletes have ever been cherished. Somehow those sentiments have been passed down from earlier generations to our own, one hundred years past the height of his racing days, and Dan Patch still holds a place in the hearts of many. In his own unique way, the crooked-legged colt from Indiana is still beating the clock.

# Notes

Many details about the careers of M. W. Savage and Dan Patch can be found in *The Racing Life of Dan Patch 1:55*, by M. W. Savage, (1914, Minneapolis); and *The Great Dan Patch*, by Fred Sasse (3rd edition, Blue Earth: 1972.) Information about Dan's first owner and early years in Indiana is available in *The Dans...and One Was a Pacer*, by Mary Cross, (1984: Oxford, Indiana).

## Prologue

1  *Minneapolis Journal*, Jan. 5, 1903.
2  For details about the scandals see Jack El-Hai, "The Shame of Minneapolis," *Mpls/St Paul* magazine, February 1992, 43; Lincoln Steffens, "The Shame of the Cities," in *The Shame of the Cities* (New York, 1904) 63-97.
3  For comments about Dan's arrival see *Minneapolis Journal*, December 8, 1902 and January 5, 1903.
4  *The Minneapolis Tribune*, January 9, 1903.
5  "Depicting Dan Patch," John Hervey, *Hoofbeats*, April 15, 1936, 507.
6  Details on the life of "Fish" Jones are from James Erlandson, *Mpls/St Paul Magazine*, April 1981, 122-125.

## 1: Dan's Debut

1  Savage, *Dan Patch 1:55*, 10-11.
2  See "Depicting Dan Patch," John Hervey, April 22, 1936; and *The Dans*, 2.
3  Hiram Woodruff, *The Trotting Horse in America*, 52.
4  Hoofbeats Magazine, "Lost in the Pages of History," John R. Stiles, September, 1976, 100.

## 2: Harness Racing: a Backward Glance

1. Details about harness racing in the nineteenth century can be found in *The New Revised Complete Book of Harness Racing*, by Philip Pines (1973); *Driver's Up: The Story of American Harness Racing*, by Dwight Akers, (1938: Putnam) and "The First Modern Sport in America: Harness Racing in New York City," by Melvin Adelman, from *The*

*Sporting Image: Readings in American Sport History* (ed. Zingg, U Press of America, 1988).

2. see Adelman, 112-118.

3. Pines, 34.

### 3: The Grand Circuit

1. Savage, *Dan Patch 1:55*, 13.

2. "Depicting Dan Patch", The Harness Horse, April 22, 1936.

3. The details of Dan Patch's season described here come from Savage, *Dan Patch 1:55.*)

4. *The New York Times*, Dec. 9, 1902, 9.

5. Savage, *Dan Patch 1:55*, 22.

6. Hervey, "Depicting Dan Patch," 542.

7. Cross, *The Dans*, 56.

### 4: The Sporting World

1. Douglas Noverr and Lawrence Ziewacz. The Games They Played: Sports in American History, 1865-1980 (Chicago, 1983) 11.

2. Pines, *Harness Racing*, 178.

3. Akers, *Drivers Up*, 257.

4. See Hervey, "Depicting Dan Patch," 542; *The New York Times*, Dec. 9, 1902, 6; *The New York Times*, April 13, 1902, 11; Akers, *Drivers Up*, 255.

5. Savage, *Dan Patch 1:55*, 16.

6. Akers, *Drivers Up*, 27-28.

7. Savage, *Dan Patch 1:55*, 1.

### 5: Mr. Savage

For details on Savage's business career see Willis Ackerman, *Dan Patch: Mass Merchandiser* (Osseo, 1981) and *Dan Patch/ M. W. Savage Update* (Osseo, 1984).

1. *Minneapolis Journal*, Dec. 3, 1901, 6.

2. *Minneapolis Journal*, Jan. 3, 1902, 6.

3. Hervey, "Depicting Dan Patch," The Harness Horse, April 15, 1936, 507.

4. Horace B. Hudson, "A Half-Century of Minneapolis," (1908),

414; *St. Paul Pioneer Press*, July 18, 1916, 1.

5. See Presbey, Frank, *The History and Development of Advertising*, (Doubleday, 1929) 294-296;   Anderson, Ann, *Snake Oil, Hustlers and Hambones* (2000), 37-38.

## 6: Three Feeds for One Cent

1. Savage, *Dan Patch 1:55*, 104.
2. Theodore Blegen, *Minnesota, A History of the State*, 391.
3. David Cohn, *The Good Old Days*, (Simon and Schuster,1940), 491.
4. *Minneapolis Journal*, August 3, 1903, 7.

## 7: Against the Clock

1. Pines, *The Complete Book of Harness Racing*, 45.
2. *Minneapolis Journal*, May 13, 1903, 2.

## 8: Our State Fair...”

1. Marling, Karal Ann, *Blue Ribbon, A Social and Pictorial History of the Minnesota State Fair*, (Minnesota Historical Society, 1990) 61.
2. *Minneapolis Daily News*, Sept. 1904, 1.
3. McCarr, Ken, “The Immortals: Marion W. Savage,” *Hoofbeats*, March 1977, 114.
4. *Minneapolis Tribune*, August 30, 1903, 5.
5. *Minneapolis Journal*, September 2, 1903, 2.
6. *The St. Paul Globe*, September 1, 1903, 2.
7. Ibid.

## 9: Good Enough for a Buggy Horse

1. Akers, *Drivers Up*, 262.
2. Ibid, 220.
3. *Minneapolis Journal*, September 28, 1903, 1-2.
4. Ibid., October 23, 1903, 8.
5. Savage, *Dan Patch 1:55*, 23.

## 10: Doomed to an Early Death

1. *Minneapolis Journal*, August 9, 1902, 6.
2. Ibid., July 21, 1904, 4.
3. Ibid., January 9, 1906, 6
4. *New York Times*, March 6, 1908, 6.

5. See *Minneapolis Journal*, Oct. 3, 1901, 1; Oct 19, 1906, 6; May 30, 1900, 3; August 20, 1902, 14.

6. Ibid., December 21, 1901, 9.

7. Ibid., March 9. 1907, 4.

8. Hersey, "The Harness Horse," May 8, 1940, 250.

9. Savage, *Dan Patch 1:55*, 103.

10. Martin, D. R., "The Most Wonderful Horse in the World," *American Heritage*, July/August 1990, 99.

## 11: National Pet

1. See for instance, Pines, *The Complete Book of Harness Racing*, 43.

2. *New York Times*, October 11, 1903, 10.

3. thewesleychurch.org/histoy/dan_patch

4.  Savage, *Dan Patch 1:55*, 29.

## 12: The Alexander of the Horse World

1. *St. Paul Pioneer Press*, September 5, 1905.

2. For details see *Minneapolis Tribune*, State Fair Scrapbook, September 7, 1905.

3. Savage, *Dan Patch 1:55*, 31.

4. Ibid., 112.

5. Akers, *Drivers Up*, 263.

## 13: The Franchise

1. Savage, *Dan Patch 1:55*, 31.

2. *Minneapolis Journal*, April 11, 1911, 11.

3. *Hoofbeats*, February 1968, 63.

4. *Hoofbeats*, January 1955, 88.

5. Savage, *Dan Patch 1:55*, 60.

## 14: Dan Patch 1:55

1. *Minneapolis Tribune*, September 4, 1906.

2. Ibid.

3. Savage, *Dan Patch 1:55*, 54.

4. *Hoofbeats*, January 1955, 90.

5. Harrison, *Autobiography*, 8.

## 15: Railroad Magnate

1. *Minneapolis Journal*, April 4, 1908, 1.

2. Ibid., May 26, 1908, 6.

3. Ibid., June 20, 1908, 6.

4. Ibid, June 25, 1908, 1.

5. *Hoofbeats*, February 1968, 63.

6. *Minneapolis Journal*, March 19, 1907, 1.

7. *Northfield News*, December 3, 1910, 1.

8. Harrison, M. E., *Autobiography of Dan Patch*, 10.

9. Hersey, "The End of the Epic," *The Harness Horse*, May 8, 1940.

10. Harrison, *Autobiography of Dan Patch*, 154-156.

11. *Hoofbeats*, March 1977, 116.

12. See Sasse, *The Great Dan Patch*, 2-9.

## 16: Trains, Horses, and Automobiles

1. For the use of horses during WWI see *Current Opinion*, August 1917, 128; *Colliers*, September 11, 1915, 34.

2. *Minneapolis Tribune*, November 19, 1916, 1.

3. *Minneapolis Journal*, November 19, 1916, 1.

4. Olson, Russell L., *Electric Railways of Minnesota* (1976), 507.

5. *Minneapolis Journal*, November 19, 1916, 1.

6. Letter from M.W. Savage to Chas. C. Lively, January 14, 1914, from the collection of George Augustinack.

7. Faribault Paper, July 19, 1916.

## 17: Last Laps

1. *Pioneer Press*, July 12, 1916.

2. *Minneapolis Tribune*, July 13, 1916, 1.

4. *Minneapolis Journal*, November 19, 1916, 1.

5. Olson, Russell L., *The Electric Railways of Minnesota*, 507.

# Dan Patch's Racing Record

## 1900 (4 year old)

| Date Place | Heat | Mile Time | Place | Purse |
|---|---|---|---|---|
| 8/30 Boswell, IN | 1 | 2:24 ½ | 1 | |
| | 2 | 2:22 ¼ | | |
| | 3 | 2:24 1/4 | 1 | $250 |
| 9/5 Lafayette, IN | 1 | 2:18 ½ | 2 | |
| | 2 | 2:16 | 1 | |
| | 3 | 2:19 ¾ | 1 | |
| | 4 | 2:16 ½ | 1 | $300 |
| 9/12 Crawfordsville, IN | 1 | 2:19 ¾ | 1 | |
| | 2 | 2:20 ¾ | 1 | |
| | 3 | 2:20 ½ | 1 | $300 |
| 9/21 Brazil, IN | 1 | 2:16 ¾ | 1 | |
| | 2 | 2:19 ¼ | 1 | |
| | 3 | 2:17 ¼ | 1 | $400 |

## 1901 (5 year old)

| Date Place | Heat | Mile Time | Place | Purse |
|---|---|---|---|---|
| 7/10 Windsor, ON | 1 | 2:07 ½ | 1 | |
| | 2 | 2:10 | 1 | |
| | 3 | 2:09 | 1 | $600 |
| 7/17 Detroit, MI | 1 | 2:08 ¼ | 1 | |
| | 2 | 2:08 | 1 | |
| | 3 | 2:09 ¾ | 1 | $2500 |
| 7/23 Cleveland, OH | 1 | 2: 10 ½ | 1 | |
| | 2 | 2:11 ½ | 1 | |
| | 3 | 2:11 ½ | 1 | $2500 |
| 7/29 Columbus, OH | 1 | 2:10 ¼ | 1 | |
| | 2 | 2:11 ¼ | 1 | |
| | 3 | 2:12 ¾ | 1 | $2000 |

## 1901 (continued)

| Date | Place | Heat | Mile Time | Place | Purse |
|------|-------|------|-----------|-------|-------|
| 8/8 Buffalo, NY | | 1 | 2:17 ¼ | 1 | |
| | | 2 | 2:10 ¾ | 1 | |
| | | 3 | 2:14 ¼ | 1 | $2000 |
| 8/16 Brighton Beach, NY | | 1 | 2:09 | 4 | |
| | | 2 | 2:04 ½ | 1 | |
| | | 3 | 2:07 ¼ | 1 | |
| | | 4 | 2:05 ¾ | 1 | $1500 |
| 8/22 Readville. MA | | 1 | 2:07 ¾ | 1 | |
| | | 2 | 2:08 ¼ | 1 | |
| | | 3 | 2:10 ½ | 1 | $3000 |
| 8/30 Providence, RI | | 1 | 2:04 ¾ | 1 | |
| | | 2 | 2:07 | 1 | |
| | | 3 | 2:06 ½ | 1 | $1500 |
| 9/5 Hartford, CT | | 1 | 2:08 ¾ | 1 | |
| | | 2 | 2:08 ¾ | 1 | |
| | | 3 | 2:12 ¼ | 1 | $3000 |
| 9/21 Cincinnati, OH | | 1 | 2:09 ½ | 1 | |
| | | 2 | 2:07 | 1 | |
| | | 3 | 2:11 | 1 | $3000 |
| 10/8 Lexington, KY | | 1 | 2:05 ½ | 1 | |
| | | 2 | 2:05 | 1 | |
| | | 3 | 2:07 ¼ | 1 | $3000 |
| 10/22 Memphis. TN | | 1 | 2:05 | 1 | |
| | | 2 | 2:06 ½ | 1 | |
| | | 3 | 2:08 ½ | 1 | $3000 |

## 1902 (6 year old)

| Date | Place | Heat | Mile Time | Place | Purse |
|------|-------|------|-----------|-------|-------|
| 7/8 Windsor, ON | | 1 | 2:06 ½ | 1 | |
| | | 2 | 2:10 | 1 | $700 |
| 7/17 Detroit. MI | | 1 | 2:05 | 1 | |
| | | 2 | 2:05 ½ | 1 | $1500 |

| Date    Place | Heat | Mile Time | Place | Purse |
|---|---|---|---|---|
| 7/22 Cleveland, OH | 1 | 2:03 ¾ | 1 | |
| | 2 | 2:05 ¼ | 1 | $1500 |
| 8/2  Columbus, OH | Exh. | 2:00 ¾ | | |
| 8/14 Brooklyn. NY | Exh. | 2:00 ¾ | | |
| 8/23 Readville, MA | Exh. | 2:00 ¼ | | |
| 8/29 Providence. RI | Exh. | 1:59 ½ | | |
| 9/4  Philadelphia, PA | Exh. | 2:00 | | |
| 9/11 Syracuse, NY | Exh. | 2:00 ½ | | |
| 9/16 New York, NY | Exh. | 2:02 ½ | | |
| 9/23 Readville, MA | Exh. | 1:59 ¼ | | |
| 10/6 Cincinnati, OH | Exh. | 2:03 | | |
| 10/8 Terre Haute, IN | Exh. | 2:01 | | |
| 10/16 Davenport, IA | Exh. | 2:01 | | |
| 10/24 Memphis, TN | Exh. | 2:01 | | |
| 10/28 Memphis. TN | Exh. | 2:01 ½ | | |
| 11/1 Memphis, TN | Exh. | 2:00 ¾ | | |

## 1903 (7 year old)
### All appearances were exhibitions.

| Date Place | Time | Purse |
|---|---|---|
| 7/17 Columbus, OH (1/2 mile) | 0:57 ¾ | $200 |
| 8/5 Erie, PA | 2:09 | |
| 8/12 New York, NY | 2:00 ¼ | |
| 8/19 Brooklyn, NY | 1:59 | $2500 |
| 8/27 Readville, MA | 2:00 ½ | |
| 9/5 Hamline, MN | 2:00 | |
| 9/7 Lima, OH | 2:04 | |
| 9/10 Hartford, CT | 2:01 | |
| 9/23 Columbus, OH | 1:59 ½ | |
| 10/1 Cincinnati, OH | 2:01 ¾ | |
| 9/18 Readville, MA | 2:00 | |

## 1903 (7 year old)

| | |
|---|---|
| 10/16 Lexington, KY | 1:59 ¼ |
| 10/22 Memphis, TN | 1:56 ¼ |
| 10/27 Memphis, TN | 1:57 ¼ |
| 10/27 Memphis, TN (1/2 mile) | 0:56 |
| 11/6 Birmingham, AL | 2:04 ¼ |
| 11/10 Birmingham, AL | 2:03 ¼ |
| 11/30 Macon, GA (2 miles) | 4 :17 |
| 11/30 Macon, GA | 2:04 ¾ |

## 1904 (8 year old)

| | |
|---|---|
| 8/30 Lincoln, NE | 2:05 ¼ |
| 10/7 Springfield, IL | 2:04 |
| 10/24 Memphis, TN | 2:00 ¼ |
| 10/26 Memphis, TN | 1:56 |
| 11/17 Oklahoma City, OK | 2:03 |
| 11/24 Dallas, TX | 2:01 |

## 1905 (9 year old)

| | |
|---|---|
| 9/4 Hamline, MN | 1:59 ½ |
| 9/9 Hamline, MN | 1:57 ½ |
| 9/13 Indianapolis, IN | 2:00 ½ |
| 9/21 Allentown, PA | 2:01 |
| 9/21 Allentown, PA | 2:05 |
| 9/30 Chicago, IL | 2:01 ½ |
| 10/5 Lexington, KY | 1:56 |
| 10/7 Lexington, KY | 1:55 ¼ |
| 10/13 Lexington, KY | 1 :59 ¼ |
| 10/21 Toronto, ON | Unknown |
| 11/1 Memphis, TN | 2:00 |
| 11/3 Memphis, TN | 1:59 ¼ |
| 11/8 Memphis, TN | 2:00 |
| 11/11 Memphis, TN | 1:58 |
| 8/22 Galesburg. IL | 1:57 ¾ |
| 8/29 Dubuque, IA | 1:58 |

| 9/4 Hamline, MN | 1:56 ½ |
| 9/4 Hamline, MN (Disallowed) | 1:55 |
| 9/19 Allentown, PA | 2:05 ½ |
| 10/2 Springfield, IL | 1:59 ¼ |
| 10/8 Lexington. KY | 1:58 |
| 10/20 Birmingham, AL | 1:59 ¼ |

### 1907 (11 year old)

| 7/25 Terre Haute, IN | 2:02 ¼ |
| 7/31 Decatur, IL | 2:01 ½ |
| 8/8 Pekin, IL | 2:03 ¼ |
| 8/15 Galesburg. IL | 1:56 ¾ |
| 8/28 Dubuque. IA | 2:00 ½ |
| 9/2 Hamline, MN | 1:58 ¼ |
| 11/11 Phoenix, AZ | 1:57 ¾ |
| 11/15 Phoenix, AZ | 1:57 ½ |

### 1908 (12 year old)

| 9/8 Detroit, MI | 1:58 3/8 |
| 9/24 Columbus, OH | 1:58 |
| 10/6 Lexington, KY | 1:57 ¼ |

### 1909 (13 year old)

| 8/10 Springfield, OH | 2:08 ½ |
| 10/4 Sedalia, MS | 2:07 |
| 11/2 Shreveport, LA | 2:09 |
| 11/9 Phoenix. AZ | 2:03 ¼ |
| 11/15 Phoenix. AZ | 2:02 ¼ |

Information derived from *The Great Dan Patch*, by Fred Sasse (3rd edition, Blue Earth: 1972.

# Index